CATCH THE WIND

FROM THE NULLARBOR TO THE FAR NORTHWEST IN '68

BRUCE LOWERY

Catch the Wind – From the Nullarbor to the Far Northwest in '68

By Bruce Lowery

© 2024 Bruce Lowery

www.brucelowery.com

Hembury Books

All rights reserved. No portion of this book may be reproduced in any form without permission from the author and publisher, except as permitted by Australian copyright law.

Cover photo supplied by the author.

CONTENTS

About the Author	v
Preface	ix
Prologue	xiii
1. The Catalyst	1
2. The Adventure Begins	11
3. The Nullarbor Blues	30
4. New Chums	45
5. Macka	67
6. Go West Young Man	81
7. Workin' and Flirtin'	96
8. Enter Big Bob	122
9. Yaringa	141
10. Chasing Jumbuck	151
11. No Bludgin'	169
12. Killing Time	184
13. An Unfair Whack	193
14. Back Down South	204
15. Hard Yakka Again	214
16. Carnaby Street Aussie Style	223
17. Casanova	236
18. Tempting Fate	244
Postscript	251
Acknowledgments	253
Also by Bruce Lowery	255

ABOUT THE AUTHOR

Bruce Lowery emigrated from the United Kingdom to Melbourne in 1955 with his parents, Bob and Effie Lowery, and his elder brother, Bob Junior.

After a brief stay with relatives in Clayton, the family moved to Victoria's beautiful Dandenong Ranges, where Bruce has had the good fortune to live ever since.

Following the late 1960s adventures described in this book, Bruce accepted a position as office boy with the Australian arm of the German/Belgian imaging company Agfa where he eventually rose to the position of National Sales Manager. Over a 37-year period, he was involved in varied Australian industries, including motion pictures, music recording, medical and industrial x-ray imaging and printing.

Away from work, Bruce is a Life Member of the Olinda Ferny Creek Football Netball club having enjoyed many positions that include player, coach, president, secretary and lately, the chair of the Sports Management Group.

He is the proud father of two much-loved daughters and grandfather to three wonderful granddaughters. He remains happily married to his wonderful wife of over 50 years, Sue.

Source: Freepik

This book is dedicated with love to my wife, Sue, who helped me rebuild the pieces all those years ago.

PREFACE

It's funny how some memories never fade. For me, it was 1968. It began with a personal heartbreak that caused me to up stumps and travel with a mate across the country to the Nullarbor Plain and beyond. Although I returned to my normal life in Melbourne and went on to have a successful and rewarding sales career, I never could forget 1968.

The opportunity for writing this book eventually surfaced when I finally retired. The time available was also made more plentiful through the lockdowns of the early COVID pandemic. Indeed, it wasn't until I finished writing that I realised I had actually written *two* books; such was the richness of my memories.

Australia in the late sixties was considerably different to the Australia that exists today. Conversely, some things remain remarkably unchanged: a high import placed on genuine mateship, and a desire for adventure amongst our young.

One of the most significant facts to consider while reading this book is that the Australian population in 1968 was about 12 million, which at the time of writing this book, has grown to around 26 million. It will also be helpful for the reader to remember that 1968 was a period before most of today's technologies existed. It was a time before we had (amongst many other things) the internet, smart phones, personal computers, and credit cards. Consequently, the ability to communicate through texts or emails simply didn't exist, and that most financial transactions were conducted in cash, money orders or cheques. The value of one 1968 dollar today is $8.64.

Air travel was too expensive to be used as a mode of travel by anyone but the very wealthy. A good percentage of homes in Australia had yet to connect to a telephone land line, so calls were often made and received from public telephone boxes. Indeed, the extremely high cost of making such calls over a long distance meant that I never once called home in all my travels from the period. Apart from the cost, I would have had to ring a neighbour to go and fetch them, as my parents were one of those families without a telephone at our home in Sassafras, Victoria.

One significant factor of note for the sixties was the introduction of the birth control 'pill' in Australia in 1961. According to many pundits this medical breakthrough introduced an era of unprecedented promiscuity amongst the younger generation. Indeed, this was often true. Previously females (and some males) had understandably been reticent to engage in any form of sexual activity because of the potential of unwanted pregnancies. The net result was that many felt less inhibited which heralded in a more 'freewheeling' attitude towards the possibilities of sexual encounters. The term 'The Swinging Sixties' was coined for good reason. On the flipside of this development, it should be acknowledged that many older Australians had been brought up with a strict 'no sex before marriage' moral code that had previously been encouraged, if not enforced, by many religious bodies and society in general. It was therefore hardly surprising that many parents were appalled by this permissive trend, and that many of them took to enforcing even harsher restrictions on their teenage sons and more particularly their daughters.

All of the above may go some way to understanding some of the 'racier' stories contained in this memoir which could easily be misinterpreted as males harassing females. For the most part the reality, as I remember it, was that in many cases both sexes were feeling pretty liberated and acted accordingly, particularly those in their late teens and twenties. Nevertheless, with the benefit of hindsight, I can see that our attitude and behaviour at times as males back then could easily be viewed today as bordering on misogynistic. Regardless, I have chosen to recount these episodes as they actually happened and beg the reader's pardon if they offend.

As I was writing this book, several friends asked me how I could remember details from events that happened over fifty years ago. It was a fair question. The answer partially lies in the fact that there were diaries to remind me. These documents ranged from relatively detailed musings to admittedly sketchy notes, but they provided several distinctly helpful things to me as a writer. They guided the verbal narrative and helped me keep the sequence of events roughly in order. They also provided me with a clear and accurate reminder of the *spirit* with which my mates and I embraced the challenges of the adventures we were experiencing, and the firm friendships and bonds we shared.

I was also fortunate to receive many letters from family and friends while travelling, and somehow, I've been able to keep most of them. They were largely written with fine clarity and filled with love; so much so that I have often quoted excerpts from them. I believe they provide an additional historical and emotional backdrop to that period of my life. Incidentally, such was the frequency of the letter writing from my mother that she often headed them with the day of the week, but not the date.

Thank goodness I kept the envelopes which were date stamped giving me the letters in a chronological date order. It's interesting to note that back then a five cent stamp allowed letters to travel to virtually any address in Australia.

Many readers may be dismayed by the frequent episodes of alcohol consumption (almost always beer, back then), but that was the reality of the times, particularly among young guys working and playing hard. Most of the time, our rather narrow focus was on having fun, listening to music, drinking beer, smoking, and chasing girls (not necessarily in that order). Fortunately, most of us matured a little as we got older.

Although I've used actual names for most of the characters in this book, I have with a nod to sensitivity, used pseudonyms for others. Throughout, I have tried to convey the experiences through the eyes and mind of an 18-year-old youth and have attempted to convey the humour, pathos and sheer fun of the events covered in these adventures. While actual conversations are necessarily paraphrased, I've made every attempt to ensure that all circumstances are consistent with actual events, and above all, the spirit of that time.

Regardless of the decade you grew up in, I hope you will be transported back to a magical time in Australian history; a time when I had some of the most remarkable experiences of my life.

PROLOGUE

I stared back through the gathering darkness from the bottom of Coonara Road towards the township of Monbulk, which was nestled in the foothills of the Dandenong Ranges. It was a bleak mid-August evening in 1968 and my heart felt as though it would burst with grief. Twelve months! Twelve fucking months without her! I had just spent every minute of the last 18 months either being with her or planning ways to be by her side. This was unbearable!

I turned and trudged slowly towards old Red Hill Road, gulping in the cold night air. The unique Dandenong Ranges combination of moist eucalyptus and other bush scents seemed to steady my mind a bit. If I used this unsealed track, it would considerably shorten the almost nine-kilometre uphill walk back home to Sassafras in the dark. At least the long, lonely walk would give me time to think. I pushed down hard on the emotions that I felt were about to overwhelm me and tried to work out what the hell had happened over the past week. I was in an utter state of disillusionment and despair.

Trish and I were both 18, had been 'going steady' for over eighteen months, and as is the case with many first loves, the relationship was all-consuming. During the early months that we dated there was great respect for each other, limiting our libidos to passionate kisses and embraces. And then, after many months, a couple of lines in a letter had unleashed a flood of passionate sexual activity that took place wherever and whenever the opportunity presented itself. I had no car, so my attic bedroom above the garage at home proved a valuable resource. The fever that had hold of each of us burned so deep that we had found ourselves in each other's arms at every opportunity, and in almost every discreet location we could find. The intensity of our love for each other had completely taken over our lives.

I forced my mind back to the previous Saturday morning…

1

THE CATALYST

Trish had met me at my place in Sassafras as arranged, so we could hitch a ride with friends to go to the local footy match. It was a bright though wintry Saturday morning, and I was playing my first season with the Olinda Ferny Creek senior football team and doing okay. Playing as a second-string ruck rover to the coach Peter 'Wacker' Jones had taught me a great deal, and I was looking forward to participating that day, as a prelude to the following weekends semi-final match in the Eastern Districts Football League. We began the short walk to the Harris's for our lift.

Something had been wrong though. Trish seemed dispirited. Her usual impish humour and cheekiness just wasn't there that morning. Her diminutive body that usually vibrated with energy and life had been replaced with stooped shoulders and a listless step. I pressed her repeatedly. 'What's wrong?' 'Are you sick?' Eventually she tried to explain. At first the words wouldn't come, her mouth opening and then shutting as she hesitated. But then the words came out in a torrent. 'I went for a ride with a guy last night, and he raped me'.

I stood thunderstruck with a wild anger welling up inside.

'Who is he?' 'Why did you go out with him?' Her half answers came in floods of tears forcing me to check myself. 'Let's go on the Harris's'. My mate Steve's dad George would know what to do.

My respect for George Harris, and his wife Nance was considerable. Stalwarts of the footy club, Nance had a solid and balanced view of the world, whilst George also had a terrific sense of humour that often lightened up difficult situations. However, when presented with our story he became unusually serious. 'Let's stop and think about this before we decide what to do,' he said quietly. 'I suggest that you Bruce still come along and play the game today, and your lovely lady can sit in the car with Nance and I to watch'.

I played, but hardly touched the ball all day. I couldn't get the images out of my mind. After showering I jumped back in the car. 'We've had a good chat,' George greeted me. 'We've decided to take you both up to the Olinda Police Station to see my mate who's in charge there. He's a good bloke and will know the best course of action to take'.

Trish and I stood in front of the friendly face of the local copper. He listened carefully as I told him the limited amount I knew. 'Okay young man,' he stated. 'This is a serious matter, and I'll need to take a statement from your girlfriend alone. You can wait outside'. My protests to stay were turned down with a friendly but firm rebuttal, so I went outside to wait... and to wait.

The Senior Sergeant finally emerged from the police station after what seemed an eternity and walked towards me. 'Listen young fellow, there's more to this situation than meets the eye. I'm going to drive Trish back to her parent's place to have a chat now. I suggest you just go home and cool your heels for a bit. Ring me at the station tomorrow afternoon and I'll have more news for you then'. He was a good local copper who I respected enormously, so I reluctantly agreed. I walked around to Falls Road to my close mate Gil's house. Fortunately he was home. There was nothing else to do but to go down to the Mt Dandenong pub to talk and drown my sorrows.

I woke up the next morning in my 'loft' bedroom nursing a very thick head. Getting drunk hadn't helped the situation one jot. I was totally miserable. I walked up to the Sassafras main street to the public telephone booth and rang her number. 'Is Trish home', I asked?'

'She's not available', was the swift reply, and the phone went dead. After a few minutes feeling totally at sea, I picked up the phone again and rang Trish's girlfriend Sonya. I explained discretely that Trish and I were in a pickle, with her parents stopping me speaking to her, and that the problem appeared to have been caused by her going out with someone else on Friday night. Did she know who HE was? I needed to know so I could sort this mess out. After some hesitation Sonya gave me a name. 'He lives somewhere down near Malvern' she said. 'Please don't do anything silly. Trish loves you. You'll be able to sort this out I'm sure'.

I walked back home and made a slice of toast that proved difficult to swallow. I decided not to explain anything about the situation to my parents. Dad had had a bad nervous breakdown several years before, and after spending a good deal of those years in Larundel Mental Asylum, he now appeared to be making a good recovery. He'd returned to his old job selling encyclopedias okay, and I didn't want to cause him any undue stress. Likewise, my caring and loving mum had my four considerably younger siblings to care for, so I figured she had enough on her plate already.

I walked back to the phone box and rang the number for the Olinda Police Station and was promptly put through to the Senior Sergeant. 'I had a long chat with your girl's parents yesterday and we all think that you and she should have a break from each other for awhile', he said.

'What about the bastard who raped her?' I said angrily. 'When are you going to charge him?'

'Not just yet just leave all that to us', replied the sergeant. I went on to explain that her family had hung up on me and were blocking me from seeing her at all. 'Look, give it a few days. I'll ask them to arrange for you to meet her and her family at the end of the week. You just need to calm down and be patient'.

I hung up with a rage building up inside that was proving difficult to control. I picked up the phone book and began to search for a name and address in Malvern.

I knocked loudly on the front door of the house in Malvern. It was opened by a youth about the same age as myself. 'Are you John Cleveland, do you know Trish from Monbulk, and did you take her out for a drive last Friday night?' I asked. 'What of it,' he sneered back. My first left hand blow to his nose was accompanied by a satisfactorily loud cracking noise. Cleveland's smug expression evaporated immediately on impact. Filled with fury I quickly followed up with a strong right hand to his solar plexus. 'Mum', he squealed through the blood that was already spurting from his nose. I let rip with two more heavy blows. 'You can't go round raping girls', I yelled at him as he slid to the ground. 'And you're a feeble prick', I added almost as an afterthought as I walked quickly back up the garden path.

I jumped into my mate Gil's car flushed with an intense feeling of exhilaration. 'Did ya get him?' Gil asked excitedly.

'You bet I did', I responded. 'He'll think twice before doing that again' I added, examining my grazed knuckles.

'The bastard got what he deserved', said Gil forcefully.

'He bloody well got off too lightly', I replied, my anger still surging inside me. We drove back to Sassafras in comparative silence. I felt somewhat reassured that my mate Gil both approved of my action, and fully supported me. That's what mates did. It was only right that unacceptable behaviour was sorted out physically, as long as it was a fair fight. He had his chance to defend himself, I told myself, but he was as weak as piss.

I took the next few days off work and withdrew into my attic bedroom feigning a head cold with my emotions alternating between extreme sadness and blinding rage. There were so many unanswered questions. Why had Trish got into a car with this guy from Malvern? Why were her parents and police preventing me from seeing her? A deep sense of foreboding began to form in my mind as anxiety started to wind its swirling tentacles throughout my brain and body.

Not knowing the real story, Mum and Dad left me to my own devices.

RETURNING TO WORK, I sat at my office desk at Masters Engineering in Bayswater. After leaving Upwey High School, I'd started as a finance clerk with the Colonial Gas Company in St Kilda Road, Melbourne, when I was 16. But I had quit and taken up a more senior position with Masters three months earlier to cut down on the commute. I found out quickly that the work was much more complex than in my previous position.

On this day, I couldn't get any of the figures to balance. I'd start each ledger entry again and again, punching the numbers into the large electronic calculator filling the paper roll with number after number, but to no avail. My mind was somewhere else. One of the accountants I reported to came over.

'How are you getting on with the payroll Bruce?' he asked.

My reply must have sounded like an incoherent ramble because he offered to take over the payroll work himself.

'Look, it's almost lunchtime. Go out and take a good long walk to clear your head'.

I took his advice and walked some distance along the side of the Mountain Highway. As I was returning to the office my step quickened. I knew what I had to do.

I stood in front of the Office Manager.

'Something bad has happened to me, sir,' I said. 'I feel that I can't cope with my work here anymore. Would you please accept my resignation, effective immediately?'

There was little doubt that the manager had been acutely aware for some time that I'd been struggling with my work in the office. There appeared to be a distinct sign of relief on his face as he agreed to my request.

Once outside I paused. Was I overreacting to the pressures surrounding me? The reflection was only fleeting. No. The world could go fuck itself! I had to clear a path to getting Trish back.

I HAD RUN hard on the training track on the Thursday night. The sheer physicality of throwing myself into every footy drill was releasing some of the frustration that was continuing to build up inside me. Coach 'Wacker' Jones urged us on. We would be playing in the first semi-final in two day's time, and he was making it clear that those who trained the hardest would be the ones most likely to retain or gain a spot in the side. Strangely for me though, I only half listened to his rhetoric on this critical training night. I was throwing myself into the training for an entirely different reason. Whilst I had always loved the game with a passion, on this night, I couldn't give a stuff if I was picked or not. I left the clubrooms straight after training finished without waiting for the selectors to announce the team.

· · ·

It was late afternoon on that brutally cold Friday when I nervously walked towards the front door of Trish's house in Monbulk. In keeping with the local copper's promise, her parents had agreed that I could visit her again. I hadn't seen or spoken with her for almost a week since that momentous visit to the Olinda Police Station. How was she? How could we sort this mess out? I'd done the right thing by reporting the matter. Surely her parents would see reason.

I was met at the door by Trish's dad. Without emotion, he ushered me into the family lounge room where Trish sat facing the wall. I stepped towards her, but suddenly her mother appeared from a shadowy corridor.

'You have caused this problem you monster', she spat at me with her eyes blazing. 'Your sinful ways have corrupted my daughter's soul. If it wasn't for you Trish would never have gone out that night with a man she hardly knew. She started to change ever since the two of you started dating.'

'That's enough Margaret,' intervened Trish's father, before turning to me. 'You have five minutes to talk with Trish', he said firmly. 'Mother and I will be staying in the room but will be over here.'

I sat down next to Trish.

'I love you,' I whispered. 'And I'll never leave you.'

She turned to me with tears welling up in her eyes.

'The police and my parents are going to force us to stay apart for 12 months,' she said quietly. 'They've told me that I have to complete my year twelve school matriculation certificate without any distractions'. She looked away. 'I had to agree. I'm so sorry'.

Her father stood up at that point, and said, 'Yes that's right. The police have stipulated that you can't see Trish for a minimum of 12 months. If at the end of that time you still feel that you love each other, you can then perhaps have limited access to her again.'

Shit, I thought to myself. Trish is the love of my life, and all they can think of me is that I'm a bad influence on their daughter, simply because we had begun a sexual relationship. Obviously, in their eyes, we had committed a mortal sin. I suddenly realised that protesting my innocence was futile, I took a deep breath.

'I'll agree,' I said standing up. 'But not because you or the damned police have demanded it. I'm only doing it because Trish has asked me to.' I bent down and gently kissed Trish on the lips whispering again. 'I love you, and I'll be here for you again in twelve months. I'll write every day'.

I left the house and began my long walk home to Sassafras. My mind whirled as I plodded slowly up the long hill. What do I do now? How could I possibly force myself to stay away from Trish for twelve whole months? The ache in my heart threatened to overwhelm me as I trudged through the cold darkening hills.

Eventually through the anguish a vague plan slowly started to form in my mind as I walked. As soon as I reached Olinda I began to walk with more purpose down the hill to Sassafras, stopping again at the public phone box. Gil answered the phone. 'Listen mate, I've got a huge favour to ask. Things haven't worked out well with Trish, so I'm leaving tonight for Perth. Could you give me lift to Melbourne now?'

After a considerable silence on the other end of the phone Gil said, 'Are you sure that's what you wanna do? It's nearly bloody 4,000 kilometres away.'

'I've never been surer of anything in my life,' I said trying to sound convincing.

'What time do you want to leave then mate?'

'In 30 minutes. I'll meet you in the main street of Sassy'.

I paused as I gathered some belongings together, stuffing them into a carry-all bag. What was I letting myself in for? Was I being stupid and rash? And then the moment of doubt left me as quickly as it arrived. What could possibly go wrong?

'Where are we heading for?' Gil asked as his old Hillman chugged its way towards town. 'Our mate Peter Lawrance is staying in Parkville at the moment, so I reckon he'll put me up for the night'. 'What did you tell your Mum and Dad mate? They must have taken the news pretty bad?', asked Gil.

'They don't know yet,' I replied. 'I've left them a note in the loft bedroom. They probably won't see it until tomorrow'. It was about 10.30 pm when we finally found the Parkville address, as Gil parked the car under a streetlight.

'You still sure you wanna go through with this mate? It's a friggin' wild idea.'

'No turning back now,' I responded.

Gil and I gave each other a hug goodbye.

'Take care mate,' was all he said before jumping back into his beloved old Hillman and driving back towards the hills.

I turned and looked at the large, terraced house. Must be a sort of guest house for students, I thought to myself. I knew that Peter had left his dad's house in Sassafras to board down here so that he could study engineering. I hadn't seen him much since the beginning of the year because of this. We had only known each other for a couple of years but had quickly found that we shared the same passion for music, starting with the pop charts, but quickly moving on to start our early exploration into blues and folk. I guess it was this, plus the fact that we each shared strongly inquisitive minds, that had led quickly into a strong friendship. I was pretty sure he would help me out with a night on his couch at short notice.

A guy in his late 20's answered the door.

'I'm afraid Peter's gone out for the night,' he said. 'I think he's gone to the movies, but you can come in and wait for him if you like'.

I was ushered into an old living room with the walls lined with hundreds of books. 'If you like reading, these will keep you entertained until Peter comes back,' my host suggested, and left the room. I picked something of interest from the shelves and settled down on a comfortable couch to wait.

I must have drifted off to sleep. I was woken by the sound of loud footsteps from an adjacent room. Might be Pete, I thought to myself as I dragged my body off the couch and walked into the kitchen. Pete had his back to me bending over the bench. I could see he was making himself a huge 'doorstopper' sandwich. He slowly turned around, lifting the sanger towards his open mouth. Before he could take a bite, his eyes met mine. 'What the hell are YOU doing here?' he asked wide-eyed.

'I've broken up with Trish, so I'm hitchhiking to Perth in the morning,' I replied with a grin. And then added optimistically, 'Wanna come?'

'Okay,' came the immediate reply.

2

THE ADVENTURE BEGINS

Our excitement over our upcoming trip was tempered when we started collating our available funds. I had a grand total of $40, but as a student, Pete only had about $10. Still, we figured we could get some work on the way if the money ran out, which we vaguely thought might happen.

'What bedding did you bring?' Pete asked.

'Nothing,' I replied. 'I've got three sets of clothes and a toothbrush'.

'You silly bugger,' Pete laughed. 'I've only got one sleeping bag, so I'll have to put in a couple of blankets into our swag too. With the money we've got, we won't be staying in any pubs or motels. We'll be sleeping rough a good bit of the time I'm guessing'.

I'd filled Pete in about my tragic situation with Trish the night before, and he took it all in with considerable sympathy, and agreed that getting away from Victoria for a while was probably a smart thing to do. He wasn't sure if studying engineering was right for him, and he could easily resume his studies after we'd had our travel adventure, if that felt right then.

'I reckon we should keep a diary of our travels,' said Pete suddenly, as he rummaged around for an exercise book.

'Good idea,' I agreed.

IT WAS a cold overcast day as we trudged out through the inner western suburbs of Melbourne, but at least it wasn't raining.

'No point in trying to hitch a ride in the suburbs,' said Pete. 'Once we get to the highway, we'll stand a better chance.'

Eventually we made it to Deer Park. Our hitch-hiking theory was that we would stand a better chance of a lift if we hitched whilst walking.

'If you stand flat-footed with your thumb out,' said Pete. 'The drivers don't think that you're serious about wanting to go somewhere'.

It sounded convincing to me, but I was wondering if his theory was sound when we had not had a lift longer than a few kilometres, and it was getting to be late in the afternoon.

Then an early model Holden skidded to a halt in front of us. We broke into a jog and were greeted by two heads poking out of the passenger side windows.

'Where ya headed guys?'

'Perth,' we said in unison.

'Christ that's a bloody long way. We better give you a lift'.

There were four guys in the car and one of them jumped from the back onto the front bench seat with two of his mates, leaving room for Pete and I to squeeze into the back with the fourth guy. We threw our bags in the boot and jumped in.

'You all look pretty happy,' I said.

'Bloody oath,' shouted the driver loudly. 'We've been to the footy and Collingwood just beat Carlton.'

'Good old Collingwood forever,' sang three of our newly

found friends, whilst the fourth sat brooding silently in the back with Pete and I.

'I guess he's a Carlton supporter,' I thought to myself, but refrained from asking him any questions. I was an elated Magpie fan too but thought it best not to rattle anyone's cage at this early stage of our lift.

The conversation about footy also brought back into sharp focus the fact that I had walked out on my own team on the very day they were playing in a final. I wondered how they had faired, but realised that a phone call from me was not likely to be well received. I'd just have to wait to find out, regardless of how guilty I felt.

'We're going all the way to Ararat,' said the driver. 'We'll get you a decent start to your trip. I hope you've got a good bit of dough because it's a fair way to Perth.'

'Well, no actually,' I said. 'We've got about 50 bucks between us, but that should get us most of the way there.'

'Geez, you're gonna have to be careful how you spend it,' he said.

'You'll need to make sure you buy the most filling food you can get,' said one of the other blokes in the front. 'Like don't go buying fish n' chips all the time. A hamburger with the lot has got much more goodness in it.' He beamed at the wisdom of his words.

After a while, the driver said, 'Look, you two look like decent blokes, so you can both kip at my place tonight if you want to. I've got a sort of granny flat out the back that nobody's using and there's a dance in Ararat tonight, so you might get lucky with the chickee babes if you go. But don't bring them back to the flat though – the missus wouldn't like that one bit.' He laughed.

Pete and I grinned and expressed our sincere thanks to these four generous souls. We'd landed on our feet on day one of the trip. It was nearly 200 kilometres from Melbourne to Ararat, and we were being offered a bed for the night, with the possibility of some country socialising when we got there. Hot damn!

Pete and I entered the impressive portals of the rather grand Ararat Town Hall at about 9.30pm and paid the one-dollar entrance fee. The rock band was in full swing, playing pop songs, with about 30 couples jigging and swaying to the beat. Strung out on seats along one wall was a long line of young blokes peering furtively across the room at an equally long line of young birds who were lined up on the seats on their side of the room. The guys were doing their best to look cool, whilst the chicks showed distinct disinterest in them. One young guy who appeared to have plucked up a considerable amount of courage walked purposefully across the divide, dodging the enthusiastic dancers as he went. He strode up to a pretty girl, grinning and pointing at the dance floor with his thumb. She shook her head and turned away to talk with her girlfriends. The poor bastard stood there for a good twenty seconds before turning, red-faced to begin the long walk back to the other side of the hall.

'Christ,' I said. 'It looks like it might be difficult getting some company tonight, Pete'.

At 10pm precisely the rock band stopped playing and announced to the crowd that it was supper time. Trestle tables appeared quickly, which were soon loaded with sandwiches, party pies, cakes and an urn full of tea.

'Now this is what I call real country hospitality,' laughed Pete.

After loading up our plates and pouring a mug of tea each, we moved to one side for others to get at the feast. But something seemed strange. The queue was mainly made up of girls, and most of the blokes appeared to have left the hall. Three or four young chicks sidled up to Pete and I.

'Where are you two guys from?' asked one.

'Not from around here, that's for sure,' added her friend with a giggle.

'We're from Melbourne,' Pete replied.

'Yeah, we guessed that,' said the first chick. 'You have longer hair, your clothes look hip, and you act real different.'

'Oh really?' I said with a smile. 'Where did all the blokes go, anyway?'

'They'll all be out there pouring as much grog down their throats as they can,' said one pretty number. 'By the time the music starts again they'll be half pissed, and no value to anyone.'

We chatted amiably enough as a few more girls wandered over to join in. At 10.30 the rock band kicked in again, and both Pete and I seemed to now have no trouble finding ready partners to dance with for the rest of the evening. Indeed, one lively young bird who I was dancing with later in the night seemed to glare at anyone else who came close to us. We grooved away to the solid beat, but precisely at midnight the band stopped playing, and somewhere from a public sound system came the unmistakable sound of 'God Save the Queen.' The sweaty couples, who had all been cavorting and throwing themselves around madly a few moments before, stopped and stood respectfully whilst the anthem was played through to the end.

It was the first time my dance partner for the last half last hour of the dance and I were able to speak coherently to each.

'My name's Linda, and I really enjoyed our groove together,' she said, smiling broadly.

'Likewise,' I replied. 'Name's Bruce. It's just good to let your hair down and go for it.' Linda then surprised me a bit by taking hold of my hand and squeezing it. 'I'm a bit worried about walking on my own past all those drunken blokes outside,' she said looking me straight in the eye. 'Any chance you could walk me home?' 'It's not that far.'

'Sure thing,' I replied. 'I'll just let my mate know that I'll see him back at our digs.'

We had walked about a kilometre out of town chatting mainly about the music and bands we liked, when Linda asked. 'What will you be doing in Perth?'

'Working hard and making a pile of dough. Might even head up north to make some serious money in the mines,' I enthused.

'What do ya want all the money for?' asked Linda.

I quickly made up an answer that I thought would be sure to impress. 'Probably go back to Melbourne to start up a rock band.'

'Would ya come back for me? I can't wait to get out of this shit hole,' moaned Linda.

'Could do,' I said trying to avoid an outright commitment so soon.

'I'm happy to show you what you would be coming back for,' Linda grinned, standing on her toes to kiss me flush on the mouth. 'Come on,' she giggled, dragging me over a fence to an open sided barn that was full of hay. She quickly lay down pulling me down too. 'Now you gotta remember that you're coming back to take me outta here.'

'I sure will,' I replied, as I reached around her back to undo her bra.

It was close to 2am when I crept silently past our host's house, quietly opening the door of the granny flat. Pete was in bed already. 'And what time of the night do you think this is?' Pete asked in a mock superior tone.

'Aw just had to see the young lady home safely, Pete,' I said.

'Never mind all that,' he intoned. 'Did you score you tinny bastard?'

'Oh, I did alright mate,' I replied vaguely.

'Prick,' said Pete, rolling over to sleep.

Pete and I were woken with a knock on the door from our amiable host.

'We'll have some breaky for you blokes in about half an hour in the kitchen,' he bellowed. 'Make yourselves lively.'

We quickly showered and made our way to our host's kitchen. 'This is the missus and the billy lids,' our host said nodding towards a smiling woman flanked by a boy and a girl about six or seven years of age.

'Welcome fellas,' she said warmly. 'There's plenty of toast on the table, and I'll make you both a brew of tea.'

'We can't begin to thank you guys enough for your kindness and trust,' piped up Pete. 'Not many people would take in two complete strangers for the night and feed them in the morning to boot.'

The missus smiled back. 'No worries fellas; it's just the way dinkum Aussies like us like to act. How was the dance last night?'

'Everyone was very friendly,' I hurriedly responded. 'It's a real nice town.'

'When you've finished feeding your faces, I'll take you to the edge of town in the car where you're more likely to pick up a lift,' chipped in the bloke of the house.

Jeepers, I thought. I'll remember this family and their kindness for a long time.

There was a bounce in our step as we marched along the highway that morning. We were nattering about nothing very important until Pete paused and looked at me seriously.

'I'm a bit confused Bruce. Just two nights ago you explained to me that you loved Trish with all your heart, that you would wait for her forever, and here we are, just one day on the road, and you're off potting the first bird you meet?' '

'Well, I really do love Trish, mate,' I said. 'But I don't intend to be totally celibate while I'm waiting 12 months to see her again. And don't forget Pete, the one that you knock back, is the one you'll never get,' I said, trying to justify what now seemed to be ill-considered actions.

'Okay, you've made your point.'

Silently though, I felt like a bit a jerk, if I was honest with myself. But then again, I reasoned, why not experience *everything* on this grand adventure?

We walked for a couple of hours towards West Stawell without a single passing car showing any inclination to stop. Just as we were starting to vent off steam about the uncaring drivers, a white Mazda slowed down and stopped about 200 metres up the road. Pete and I looked at each other a bit nonplussed as the car began to reverse back towards us. The driver leaned across the front seat and wound down the passenger side window.

'Where are you guys going?' he asked.

'Perth,' we replied.

'I'm only goin' as far as Adelaide,' he said. 'But if you two can chip in for some petrol, I'm happy to take you that far.'

'Sounds like a good deal to us,' beamed Pete as we jumped in.

'Me name's Dick Robinson,' said the driver, who appeared to be in his early thirties.

After we had introduced ourselves, the conversation barely slowed down for the next four hours. We covered subjects as diverse as girls (of course), music, cars, religion, and sex (of course, again).

I paid to top up the petrol tank at a service station as we were entering a town called Murray Bridge.

After jumping back in the car, Dick looked at both of us and said, 'All this driving and talking has given me a thirst. Who's for a beer?'

'But it's Sunday, you silly prick,' said Pete. 'Unless the laws are different in South Australia to Victoria, every bloody pub will be closed.'

'Trust me,' grinned Dick, and proceeded to drive down the road to the nearest hotel, parking the car boldly right out the front.

'Come with me boys,' said Dick with a smile. We walked through to the lounge, where a few houseguests sat chatting. Leaving us standing in the middle of the large room feeling like two stranded whales, Dick walked up to the barman and spoke quietly in his ear. The barman nodded and produced a pad.

'Just come over and sign this you guys,' said Dick. 'What'll you have?'

'A pot of beer,' Pete and I said in unison, hardly believing our eyes.

But after three pots appeared on the bar we were quickly convinced. Forbidden nectar never tasted so good.

'How did ya manage this, Dick?' I asked.

'As long as you sign a stat dec that you have travelled a certain number of miles in a day, every pub in Australia has to serve you food and drink by law.'

'Well, I'll be buggered,' announced Pete. 'That's useful to know.'

We paid for Dick's meal at the pub that night, sinking a few more beers as we finished our dinners and grinning like Cheshire cats.

'We're only about an hour from Adelaide,' Dick informed us. 'Let's get going.'

We wound our way through the Adelaide Hills until we could see the twinkling lights of a large city.

'There she is guys. The beautiful city of Adelaide,' shouted Dick, as if we had just found Treasure Island.

Dick drove us around the quiet city streets to give us a flavour of the place, eventually pulling over and stopping.

'What now?' I asked. 'We don't have enough bucks to stay in a motel or anything.'

'Me neither,' said Dick. 'It's too late to keep driving tonight, so I'll kip in the car before driving up to the Barossa in the morning to stay at my sister's place. You can kip in here too if you like. It's frigging cold out there'.

'Done deal,' agreed Pete as we all settled down to what proved to be one of the most uncomfortable night's sleep I'd ever had. There isn't much room in a small Mazda for three grown blokes.

The next morning, we slowly stretched our cramped limbs, splashed some cold water over our faces in a public toilet and brushed our teeth.

'Well, Dick,' I said. 'The least we can do is buy you breakfast.'

The rain was light but steady as we sat in a bustling Adelaide café, trying to make our tea last a bit longer, before Dick finally stirred himself.

'I'll drive you blokes to the bus depot so you can get out of town before hitching,' he offered.

Pete and I hugged the bloke hard before jumping on the bus. It's surprising how close you can get to someone in a short time. But then again, we had all slept together, hadn't we?

After arriving at Gepps Cross, we jumped off the bus and began to walk down the highway through the drizzling rain. In a valiant attempt to cheer Pete up, I began to sing a song I loved called Alice Long.

'Shit Bruce,' grumbled Pete. 'Tommy Boyce and Bobby fucking Hart. Can't you do any better than that?'

'Sorry mate, I thought it might brighten up your day,' I said. 'I'll shut up now.'

We walked on in silence. After a while Pete, began to hum to himself. I picked up the melody of the old folk tune 500 Miles, and we both started to sing, softly at first, but then with more conviction, as we found a strange rhythm that matched our mood.

We picked up a few short rides from some well-meaning locals, but it was mainly hard walking as the wind and rain picked up. We plodded on, each carrying a handle of the largest of the carry-all bags. Eventually we staggered into the town of Two Wells as the light was fading. I stood on a shop veranda shaking as I began to devour the lukewarm pie that I had managed to buy from the local store before it closed. Pete eating an equally tepid pastie. 'We've gotta find somewhere out of the rain to let our clothes dry off,' said Pete, trying not to tremble.

After polishing off our pitiful meal we started walking through the little town and got lashed by the driving wind and rain. We finally found the local state school.

'Look – there's a shed in the grounds,' shouted Pete. 'Let's see if we can get inside.' The door didn't take much forcing, and we were relieved to be out of that bloody rain. Inside it was completely dark. Pete lit a match. Loads of gym gear was stacked up in piles. Most importantly, there was a pile of old gym mats. Once we got out of our soaking clothes, it wasn't too uncomfortable.

'Night,' said Pete wiggling himself into the sleeping bag.

We both soon fell into a deep sleep.

I WOKE up to the pleasant sound of children playing. And then I remembered where the hell we were.

'Shit Pete – wake up for Christ's sake. The kids have arrived for school.'

In a mild state of panic, we stuffed our half-dried clothing, blankets and sleeping bag into our carrying bags, pushing the gym mats back into the pile they came from.

'There's nothing else we can do but open the door and make a run for it,' Pete whispered.

'Okay I'll be right behind you,' I replied.

With that, Pete pushed open the door and we made a dash for the fence.

'Look, there's two men coming out of the shed,' a young voice shrilled.

A dozen wide-eyed kids were pointing in our direction as we straddled the fence in one bound and headed for the main street of Two Wells.

'Not a great start to the day,' wheezed Pete.

'Aw, they'll get over it,' I said. 'I wonder what we can get to eat,' I added. 'I'm bloody starving.'

We stepped into a café, where the owner cooked up some hot chips and made us big paper cups of tea. I settled onto a wooden bench on the veranda to eat my breakfast, while Pete nervously kept looking back towards the school.

'Stop worrying Pete,' I began to say, but stopped mid-sentence. I could see a police car slowly driving up the main strip. It stopped about 20 metres from us.

'I think we better make ourselves scarce,' I said turning to walk the other way, but immediately saw two burly blokes in blue police uniforms coming straight towards us from the other direction.

'Righto you two,' bellowed the first cop. 'We'd like to have a word with you.'

They led both Pete and I over to the waiting police car and sat us on the back seat.

'We don't know what you blokes were playing at down at the school yard this morning so we're going to take you down to the station for some questioning.'

I offered him a hot chip.

As we were being driven to the police station, Pete leaned

over and whispered, 'You better leave the talking to me. They already think you're a bloody smartarse.'

'If you think it's for the best mate,' I agreed.

Inside the nick, Pete explained that we were hitch-hiking to Perth for work purposes, got caught in the storm, and were forced to seek shelter. He went on to say that we had intended no harm and regretted it if we had upset anyone. From where I sat it was a convincing performance, but the police still looked menacing.

'Let's see your ID,' said one of the coppers.

Peter produced his student card. As I hadn't yet applied for my driving license, I had nothing to show them, which seemed to irritate them even more.

'So why are you going to a job in Perth when you're a student?' asked one copper.

Pete then spun them a yarn about having no financial support, so he had had no alternative but to go to work in the West Australian mines for a while before returning to Melbourne to complete his studies. That seemed to have cut through a bit with the two cops.

'Well, that being the case, we'll take you over to the school to see if the headmaster wants to press charges. If he does, you'll both be held in the cell out the back until the magistrate's court hearing next week.'

I shuddered at the thought.

If I thought that Pete's explanation at the police station was good, it paled into insignificance when compared to the outstanding performance he gave to the headmaster. Pete waxed lyrical about how he had come from a large, poor family, and he'd always had to look after himself. Given the right opportunity, he would complete his studies and make something of himself.

The headmaster listened carefully, and gentle soul that he

was, sighed and said with unexpected generosity, 'Well, there appears to have been no damage done, so I don't think we need to press charges.'

The police looked relieved to have their paperwork suddenly minimised.

'Right,' they said, 'Back in the car, the two of you.'

We were driven back through the town, and out along the highway for about 10 kilometres, where they pulled the police car over.

'It's been your lucky day you two. You can now shove off, but if either of you ever step foot in Two Wells again, we'll lock you both up for a long time.'

Pete and I resumed our journey, feeling determined to put some distance between us and Two Wells. After about an hour, a shiny Holden sedan pulled over and without waiting for an invitation, we jumped in.

'Max Webber's the name, guys. Where are you heading for?' After we had explained our situation in considerable detail, Max kindly offered to take us another 300 kilometres to where he had business to attend to in a town named Whyalla.

In the meantime, would we like to guess the nature of his work? Our guesswork over the next hour could only narrow things down to the fact that Max was a salesman, but selling what? Eventually after exhausting all our ideas, Max explained that he sold trees. Plantations of trees in fact, offered to farmers who had some spare land. An investment that would not only net the farmer an eventual handsome profit in timber sales but be good for the environment as well.

We settled in for the drive, with Max impressing us with his vast knowledge about many things, but eventually it was his questions about our plans that gave Pete and I a clue about the next possible step in our grand adventure.

'So, you're running low on money, are you?' Max asked.

We nodded. This was indeed distressingly the case.

'You could always try for some factory or labouring work in Whyalla,' he said. 'But why don't you try for jobs that will actually take you closer to Perth?'

What did he have in mind?

'There's a bloody long railway line stretching all the way across the Nullarbor Plain, and the thing doesn't maintain itself.'

Pete and I looked at each other. We had never thought that something like a railway would actually need looking after.

'Yep,' Max continued. 'They're always on the lookout for fettlers. If you like the idea, I can take you to the railway station at Port Augusta to see if they would be interested in taking you on?'

'BOTH OF YOU strip down to your underpants,' ordered the rather large and stern nurse standing menacingly in front of us. The Employment Manager had indeed been very interested in the fact that we were seeking employment.

'Any objection as to where you would be located?' he had asked with a vague air.

I detected a poorly camouflaged grin when we said that as long it was closer to Perth, we were quite flexible.

'Well, if you can pass our stringent medical examination, we may have something for you,' he replied.

The nurse approached us.

'Show us your hands,' she demanded. 'Why all the blisters?' she asked suspiciously.

'It's because we've carried our bags all the way from Melbourne,' Pete responded.

This prompted a grunt from the nurse. She moved uncomfortably close, and to my enormous surprise, suddenly reached into my undies and took a firm grip of my testicles.

'Turn your head to the side and cough,' she commanded.

I acquiesced by emitting a pathetically strained vibration. She loosened her clammy grip on my crown jewels and withdrew her paw from my underclothing.

'Next,' she said, taking a couple of quick strides towards my mate.

Pete's open-mouthed look of astonishment quickly turned into one of fear. The nurse then completed the identical coup de grace on my mate with the same ruthless efficiency.

'You're both fit enough for the job,' she concluded, sending us back to the Employment Manager with a perfunctory wave of her hand.

'Well, so much for the stringent medical, Pete,' I said as we walked back to the employment office.

'She seemed to enjoy herself a bit too much,' replied Pete.

'At least you had a bit of advance warning before being assaulted,' I laughed.

'We'll get you off to O'Malley on the train tonight, fellas,' said the manager as Pete and I signed the employment contracts. 'There will be some start up food supplies there for you, and you can then top these up once your first pay packet arrives.'

'How big a town is this place, and where is it?' asked Pete.

'Oh, it's a pretty quiet and small place, but it's almost halfway to Kalgoorlie as you wanted,' replied the manager. 'You had better go and get yourself a feed now, because there's no grub on the train. Try the Hotel Commonwealth down on Commercial Road. The train leaves at 9.45 sharp, so don't be late.'

'How much dough do we have left mate?' asked Pete as we made our way in the general direction of the pub.

'Enough for a good feed, and a few beers,' I replied.

'How are you off for smokes though?' he said. 'I've only got about half a packet of Camels.'

'Shit I'm down to about half a dozen Marlboros,' I moaned.

'Let's run over to the general store to replenish before it closes,' urged Pete. 'I reckon it's time to stop smoking tailor made fags and change to roll your owns – Drum's the best I reckon.'

'Okay, but let's also get some snacks to eat on the train,' I said, thinking about my stomach as usual.

WE SAT in the Hotel Commonwealth lounge bar with another dozen or so customers. We'd both opted for the cheapest value for money meal by choosing the mixed grill, which was indeed huge, but pretty chewy for the most part. We still had an hour and a half to kill.

'Another pot?' Pete asked.

'Yeah, but I might switch from the Southwark to the Coopers though mate.'

'Good idea.'

I looked around at the other punters. They were down-to-earth country folk who seemed content to keep well away from the two longhaired hippie types sitting in the corner.

The jukebox blared out 'And the Rain Tumbled Down in July', with Slim Dusty in full voice, causing many of the punters to tap their feet in time to the music.

After the adrenaline-charged start to our adventure over the past few days, I was starting to feel a bit blue. It really was going to be 12 months before I got to see Trish again, not to mention my family and all our mates back in the hills.

Pete came back to the table carrying the two pots of beer.

'Isn't that Jim Reeves on the jukebox?' he said with obvious contempt. 'Haven't you got a couple of coins left to put on some decent music Bruce?' he added.

I nodded and plodded over to the jukebox to forlornly scan the disc titles on display. I selected a few tracks, popped in the coins, and wandered back to our table.

Pete was chattering away about the difference between Southwark and Cooper beer patently oblivious to my growing mood of sadness.

'Cooper's the better of the two,' he pronounced. 'But neither is as good as Victoria Bitter back home.' He then paused to listen to the melancholy song I had chosen.

'Did you put this on?' Pete demanded. 'Bobby bloody Goldsborough!' 'But it was Trish and my song Pete,' I said pitifully.

'Oh, okay,' said Pete. 'I'll shut up for a while.'

Soon enough we had both succumbed to melancholy. We talked about what we missed back home as the beers took advantage of our susceptible state. We reflected on close mates, families, and of course, I was thinking helplessly about Trish.

'Shit, it's nearly 9.30 mate,' Pete suddenly bellowed. 'We better run for it.' And run we did, as fast as our baggage and semi-legless state allowed. We arrived at the railway station just as the clock ticked over to 9.45 pm. I breathlessly ran over to the ticket counter.

'Where's the 9.45 to Kalgoorlie?' I yelled.

'Been delayed mate,' came the casual reply. 'Just take a seat and relax.'

Pete and I settled down to wait on a station bench seat hunched against the cold night. At around 10.30 pm a guy in a cowboy hat, boots and jeans sauntered up to the station. 'The train's running late,' Pete advised him.

'That's normal,' he replied. 'Trains on the Commonwealth Railways are always late. Reckon we'll see it around 11. Name's Bill by the way.'

'He thinks he's a bloody cowboy,' I whispered to Pete.

At 10.55 pm a train pulled into the station. Behind it were

carriage upon carriage of cattle trucks. Two passenger carriages were at the rear.

'Must be for us,' I said wearily. 'Let's get into the last one to be as far away from the cattle as possible. Shit – they stink.'

As we were about to jump in, half a dozen Aboriginals emerged from the shadows and opened the doors to the second last carriage, slipping inside quietly.

'Those fellas are only seen when they want to be seen,' announced our new mate, Bill. Moments later a whistle blew, and the train began to move.

My sadness evaporated as I thought with excitement about what lay ahead.

3

THE NULLARBOR BLUES

The train travelled at an extraordinarily slow pace and the decrepit seats were lumpy and uncomfortable. I wrapped myself in blankets while Pete wriggled into his sleeping bag. It was freezing and we were emotionally exhausted. Bill somehow fell asleep sitting bolt upright, oblivious to the cold. Pete looked over at Bill's sleeping form. 'Wanted Dead or Alive – Billy the Lid,' said Pete, grinning widely.

'More like Wild Bill Hiccup,' I snorted.

As tired as I was, my sleep was fitful. I woke several times as the train stopped and started, sometimes at small workman's' camps without name plates, and sometimes in the middle of nowhere.

Eventually the thin grey light of dawn filtered into the carriage. The view from the grubby windows revealed an endless plain dotted with small knee-high bushes, and not a tree in sight. In the hours that followed, the view barely changed at all.

Pete and I shared some chocolate from our meagre food supplies and washed it down with bottled soda water. Wild Bill snored on. The adventure was proceeding, albeit at an extremely slow pace.

The offensive smell from the five hundred or so cattle in the trucks travelling ahead of us was almost overwhelming.

'Speaks volumes about our new employers' opinions about their new workers,' said Pete glumly. 'The bloody cows are more important than us,' he added.

'I've just smoked my last Marlboro,' I said, trying to change the subject. 'Can you teach me how to roll a fag with the Drum tobacco mate?'

The regular need for the succour of nicotine made me an expert smoke roller in no time, impressing Pete, who had already mastered the art some time before.

Occasionally the train guard wandered along through the carriage nodding to us, but never speaking a word. I guessed that he was used to the long hours of solitude that went with his job, and that socialising was not high on his agenda. Wild Bill continued to snore. Man, that guy could sleep.

'He's probably dreaming about his next gunfight,' quipped Pete.

Late in the morning, the guard reappeared. I stopped him with a smile and asked, 'How's your day been?'

He paused, nodding once more.

'I was wondering if I could ask a few questions about the Commonwealth Railways?' I added.

'What do you need to know?'

'Well, we're going to be working at a place called O'Malley, so we were hoping to know a bit about the place before we got there.'

This was obviously a huge green light to the guard. He instantly changed from a recluse to a raconteur with an encyclopaedic mind.

'O'Malley is a maximum six-man camp roughly 800 kilometres from Port Augusta, and about 900 from Kalgoorlie,' he started. 'It's purely a fettlers' camp with no electricity, and the nearest made road is about 150 kilometres away down on the coast. The only way to get in and out is by train and it's pretty much smack in the middle of the Nullarbor. A little-known fact is that a load of Italian POW's worked at O'Malley and a few other camps along the line way back in 1942. There could still be a few of their ghosts wandering about out there,' he joked. 'We should be there about late afternoon, so keep your eyes peeled for Ooldea and Watson. O'Malley is the next camp after that but get all your gear ready in advance. The train will stop at O'Malley for sure, but only for a couple of minutes,' he finished, before walking back towards the guard's van.

'Christ, we really are going to be in the middle of nowhere,' said Pete apprehensively.

'It sure sounds like a barrel of laughs.'

It was just past 3 pm and I was about to nod off again when the train emitted a loud whistle. I had just partially opened my eyes when I noticed a sign with Ooldea displayed in bold letters flash past.

'Wake up,' Pete, I said with sudden excitement. 'We're almost there.'

We said our farewells to Wild Bill and got all our meagre belongings together. About 30 minutes after passing the well signposted Watson camp, the train began to slow down and came to a stop. A single signboard advertised the name of our new digs: O'Malley. It consisted of three small tin buildings, a few outer sheds, and a water tank on a tall metal tower.

We jumped out of the carriage to see two figures emerge from the hut. One bloke was no more than about five foot and a bit tall, with a large girth and strong looking arms. His mate was a slender, much taller guy. He walked behind the first fella. I guessed they were in their mid-fifties.

'What have they sent us this time,' muttered the big guy to nobody in particular.

'Lawrance and Lowery I assume,' he continued, stopping a few metres in front of us, and without waiting for a reply added,

'I'm the Ganger around here,' he said firmly. 'Ganger means boss, so do as you're told, and we'll get on fine. Couldn't find a barber before you caught the train?'

We still hadn't said a word as the Ganger turned on his heel, shouting over his shoulder, 'Danny here'll show you to your digs.'

Pete and I exchanged glances.

'Come over this way guys,' said the softly spoken Danny. 'It's good to have some new faces. The last guys left a good week or so ago. We're supposed to have six fettlers at O'Malley to keep up with the work, but with you two, we're still only four. The Ganger's name is Pete. His bark is usually worse than his bite, but he's been out here for over thirty years, so you could call him a bit of an eccentric, I suppose.'

We walked into the end hut. I stared at the sparse surroundings. A small table with a couple of wooden chairs stood in the middle of the room. There was a wood burner stove with some cheap benches either side. Off each end of the cabin was a bedroom, each with a metal-framed, sagging bed covered by a none too clean mattress and pillow. Walking back to the main room, Danny advised us that there was a start-up food ration pack in the cupboards, and to be careful with water consumption from our rainwater tank, which was only topped up when it rained, which wasn't very often. Apparently, there was plenty of water in the main header tank, which was regularly topped up by a water tanker train. It was suitable for washing but not drinking, as it was bore water.

'We have bread dropped off to us by the train every couple of days,' said Danny. 'But for most supplies we have the 'Tea and

Sugar' train stop here once a week, and the mail is picked up and delivered every couple of days. By the way, each cabin has its own dunny out the back. 'I'll see if I can steal a couple of bottles of Bock beer from the boss for you to celebrate your arrival,' Danny concluded, leaving us to wonder what the hell Bock Beer was.

'Home away from home,' I grinned to Pete.

'It's a bit of a shithole, but we'll just have to make the best of it. I think I'm going to like Danny, but what did you make of the boss?'

'Well, he's an odd shape to start with, and he certainly has a snappy way with words. The fact that his name is also Pete is going to lead to confusion, though.'

'I reckon he looks a bit like the Abominable Snowman,' laughed Pete.

'No argument there from me.'

We rummaged through the cupboards and found some stale bread plus a few cans containing beans, vegetables, spam and corned beef. I pounced on some jars of jam and vegemite.

'At least we have something to put on the bread,' I said.

'How are your cooking skills?' asked Pete.

'To be honest I even burn the tea. But I'm a mean hand at cutting firewood for the stove.'

'Well, I noticed there was plenty of old sleepers lying around out there mate, so you had better get cracking, if we're going to eat something warm tonight.' I went out and found a rusty old axe and bow saw.

Pete had worked some kind of miracle with the goods available to create a pretty darn good meal, and we washed it down with the Bock beer kindly pinched for us by Danny. 'Bock beer is just the name of a type of German style beer, but the boss has his own recipe,' said Danny.

'Cripes,' I said. 'It's bloody good.'

After we had finished eating, Pete looked over at me. 'I think we need to share the load on this trip mate.'

'What do you mean?' I said quizzically.

'Well, you know how we share the writing duties in our diary with you writing two day's worth, and then me alternating? We should do the same with the sleeping bag and the blankets. The sleeping bag is a lot warmer, so by alternating every couple of nights, the one in the sleeping bag is likely to get a better nights' kip.'

I was impressed by my friend's generous gesture, until he added, 'No wanking or farting in the sleeping bag though.' It kind of ruined the moment.

Our room had warmed up considerably, courtesy of the roaring fire in the stove, and the two kerosene lamps gave off a warm flickering glow.

'Life's not so bad after all,' I ruminated out loud. 'But I think I need a dump.'

'Better take one of the lamps,' replied Pete. 'Let me know if you bump into one of those Italian POW ghosts out there.'

I hurried outside through the freezing cold night to our designated dunny. It was wisely located quite some distance away from our sleeping quarters. I opened the dunny door, sniffing the overwhelmingly strong odour of phenyl. It only partially covered the stench of stale human excrement.

'Better than being totally overcome with the smell of shit,' I said to myself as I pulled down my daks.

There was a huge pile of Pix and People magazines, plus a few Man Illustrated for me to flick through.

As I was finishing up, the light in my lamp began to splutter as the kero started to run out. I opened the dunny door just as the flame in my lamp was extinguished completely. All of a sudden, I became aware of the huge umbrella of stars above me. I stopped walking, astounded by the brightness of the sparkling vision above me. I had never seen the night sky this highly illuminated. Spectacular hardly seemed an adequate description.

I ran back to the cabin shouting, 'Pete, Pete! Come outside, quick.'

He rushed out through the door, stopping and looking up as I stood there pointing skywards. Although it was bitterly cold that night, both of us stayed outside for quite some time, completely overawed by the experience.

THE SOUND of stones hitting the roof that morning was deafening. Pete popped his head out the door to see the Ganger standing outside.

'You've got 15 minutes to be ready for work,' commandeered our boss.

We splashed some water on to our faces, brushed our teeth, and spread a bit of jam over a piece of stale bread.

'We've just got time to make a couple of vegemite sandwiches for lunch,' I said, ramming in the last mouthful.

All four camp members gathered next to the yellow ganger's trolley. It sat on the rails, running at right angles to the actual railway line. Danny grabbed a device resembling a turntable off the back of the trolley and placed it in the middle of the main railway tracks, at which time the Ganger instructed us to manually push the trolley forward off the siding over the top of the turntable. We then spun the trolley round until it was in line with the main railway line and then simply pushed the trolley straight onto the tracks. 'Nifty,' I thought as the Snowman bellowed 'All aboard.' The petrol engine roared into life, and we took off down the line at speed.

After travelling about five or so kilometres, the Ganger slowed the trolley, stopped, and jumped off, grabbing a spirit level and flat board.

After taking note of the differing height levels of the steel railway lines, the Snowman grunted, 'This is a good spot to fix. Each of you blokes grab a beater and get yourselves over here.'

Danny passed us a tool with a lengthy wooden handle. It vaguely resembled a pick. The metal head had what looked like a very blunt hoe on one side, with two prongs on the other.

'We'll start with you, young Lowery,' the Snowman said. 'Come over here and use the two prongs to scrape out the rock ballast from between each of these 12 sleepers, inside and out: but only on this side of the line.'

I slowly began the task, hoping desperately that I understood his directive. Suddenly the Snowman was at my side, giving me a quick hip and shoulder that Polly Farmer would have been proud of. He took the beater out my hands at the same time.

'Yer nothin' but a bloody namby-pamby,' he bellowed.

His strong arms moved vigorously as he scraped out the rocks from the sleepers.

'This is how we work out here,' he said as he began to bash the rocks back under each sleeper with the blunt end of the beater. His muscular arms swung with great force. Thwack! Thwack! Suddenly it dawned on me. We were raising the level on one side of the railway line by belting the ballast rocks back under the sleepers! I accepted my beater back, and began to work again more earnestly, as Pete and Danny were shown their part of the line to work on. So this is what fettlers did for a living.

By the time 'smoko' arrived at 10 o'clock I was exhausted, with the palms of my hands covered in painful blisters. Evidently, being young and fit for an explosive game of Aussie Rules footy was not the same as being fit enough for hard labouring graft. Danny had started a fire, boiled some water, thrown in some tea leaves, and swung the billy tin around in a great circular arc, meshing the brew nicely. We all accepted our fully filled metal tin mug gratefully, and sank to the ground. A cuppa had never tasted this good before.

The work continued in this fashion throughout the day. Moving from one location to another, repeating the exercise again and again, stopping only for a half hour lunch and a 15-minute afternoon 'smoko'. Several times the Ganger took us and the trolley to pre-determined spots on the line, where we were able to once again use the turntable to move our trolley off the line into little sidings. Each time a huge train would then thunder past with passengers staring out of the windows at us. We'd then reverse the procedure with the trolley to return it the main railway line.

Late in the afternoon, as we were returning to O'Malley, the Snowman stopped the trolley to look up to the top of a long line of telegraph poles.

'Lawrance,' he bellowed. 'Shin up that pole and remove that bloody crow's nest.'

Pete dutifully shinned his way to the top and reached into the nest.

'Hey Bruce,' he called out, throwing an object down in my direction.

My sporting nature kicked in as I tried to catch it. Splat! A crow's egg makes quite a mess when it arrives at high velocity.

That night, we finished off our carefully composed letters to send back home. I took particular care with my letter to my Mum and Dad, explaining the reasons behind my sudden departure. I reread the letter to Trish that I had written the previous night and was quite satisfied. It conveyed my love to her in passionate and lurid detail. I don't know why it didn't dawn on me that her parents were likely to read it first. And that's exactly what they did.

The Snowman did his level best to show us long-haired city

boys how hard working and tough real fettlers were. The next day was much the same as the one before, but although feeling rather sore, we already sensed that we could now cope and weren't going to be beaten. Finally arriving back at our little abode, we ate our roughly put together meals in relative silence before being surprised by a knock on the door. It was Danny bearing gifts.

'It'll get easier from now on boys,' he said with a grin. 'Here are some packets of potato chips left by some of the guys who have moved on, and here are some books I've finished with too.'

We thanked this little gem of a guy wholeheartedly, quietly noting that some of the book titles looked enticing.

Selecting a paperback titled *The Naked Island* by a bloke named Russell Braddon, I retired to bed early and tried to read by the feeble light of a kerosene lamp. Although early indications that the book was obviously a well written account of the author's time as a World War 2 POW in Changi, I eventually gave up and fell into a deep sleep.

THE SNOWMAN EXPECTED us to work six days a week. We were back on the trolley again by 8am, but this time we just kept heading in a north westerly direction, eventually turning around and simply returning to O'Malley.

'Tea and Sugar's due in half an hour,' advised the Snowman.

Pete muttered under his breath, 'So, why the early morning ride for nothing?' 'Better make out a shopping list, I guess,' I mused, trying not to feel as pissed off as Pete evidently did.

As the all-important Tea and Sugar train appeared on the horizon, Danny told us that the Ganger would firstly grab our pay packets and give them to us so we could do our shopping.

'But don't hang around guys,' he added. 'She'll only be stopping for around 10 minutes, so grab a wheelbarrow to throw your shopping in. By the way, if you want some booze for next week, you'll have to throw a couple of bucks to the guard for him to get it for you'.

With a newfound sense of urgency, Pete and I pushed the wheelbarrow over to the tracks. The Tea and Sugar thundered to a stop and the Snowman wandered over to the guard's van, accepting four pay packets. I ran over and grabbed ours. Each carriage was a different shop.

'I'll go to the butchers,' shouted Pete, grabbing his pay packet from me.

I dashed over to the general provisions' carriage. After we had dumped the results of our shopping spree into the wheelbarrow, I noticed the Snowman carefully placing quite a number of cartons from the guards' van in his barrow.

'Shit, that looks like a lot of grog,' said Pete.

'Never mind that,' I yelled. 'Let's place our own bloody booze order for next week before the frigging train leaves.'

I barely had time to complete this complex transaction before the train whistle sounded, and the train moved off.

After lunch in our hut, Danny wandered in.

'It's the boss's birthday today, so he wants to know if you'll both join us for dinner,' he asked casually.

To say that both Pete and I were surprised was quite an understatement.

'Umm okay,' Pete said.

'See you at seven then,' said Danny, and he sauntered away.

Who would have guessed?

As soon as we arrived at the boss's place, we were each handed a long-necked bottle of Bock beer. The Snowman had a lop-sided grin on his face, clearly having had a head's start on us. Danny had prepared a most satisfactory meal, which we all wolfed down. The night proceeded with the Snowman providing us with many pearls of wisdom about what it took to become a real man. No problem for us. As long he kept taking the tops off more bottles of his magnificent beverage, we'd be happy to listen to the Snowman's increasingly incoherent advice. In fairness, by around 11 pm, all four of us were babbling and chuckling in an increasingly advanced state of happy inebriation.

We awoke late with very thick heads, but the luxury of enjoying several Weet-Bix and some sugar, soaking in a metal cup of warm water, pepped me up considerably. Sunday meant no work, so we took the opportunity to wash our grubby clothes after being shown a nine-gallon copper boiler in the laundry by Danny.

'Just get a good fire going, pop in your clothes when she's boiling, and stir them around for bit,' advised Danny.

'You can scrub your gear a bit with a bar of Sunlight soap, if they're really dirty,' he finished.

We set to with the job, quietly impressed by how clean everything turned out.

By early afternoon we still hadn't sighted the Snowman, but later in the day we spotted our boss with a bottle in his hand again.

'I think you and I had more than enough booze last night, without drinking any more today,' noted Pete.

'Doesn't seem to worry the Snowman,' I replied. 'In any case, we don't have any more booze until the Tea and Sugar arrives next Saturday.'

'Yeah,' replied Pete. 'I don't expect the Snowman to be all that generous again with his Bock beer. Anyhow, I'm going to get started making a stew now. I bought two kilos of diced lamb and loads of veggies yesterday, so I'll make enough to last the rest of the week.'

'Not bloody stew every day,' I protested.

'Look mate. There is no fucking fridge at O'Malley, and even if there was one, there is no damn electricity, so we have to cook all our meat within a couple of days of buying it. A cooked stew will keep for five or six days no problem.'

'If you say so,' I replied without much enthusiasm.

THE ROCKS LANDED on the roof of our luxury unit again in the morning, but considerably later than usual. All four residents of O'Malley eventually gathered at the trolley about mid-morning. The Snowman didn't say much and was looking decidedly pale. We all jumped aboard the trolley and took off travelling for about 12 or so miles, and then turned around and headed back to O'Malley.

'Not well,' muttered the Snowman. 'I'll see you blokes tomorrow.'

Having most of the day off gave Pete and I plenty of time for reflection. I hoped that my letter to my folks had adequately explained my reasons for leaving home so abruptly. I didn't want them worrying.

My parents Bob and Effie had emigrated, with my older brother Bob 'Junior' and I from England to Australia in 1955 as 'Ten Pound Poms', eventually settling into a small house near Belgrave one year later. My parents had restarted having kids again about four years after that, eventually producing three more sons and one daughter. Geoff, Sue, Johnny and Mick were between eight to thirteen years younger than myself, and although they were all good kids, they were quite a handful for my dear old Mum. To add to her difficulties, Dad's mental health was still delicate following a severe nervous breakdown in 1964. He did appear to be finally improving, at least. My older brother Bob had been called up for two years of National Service and was currently based at Puckapunyal near Seymour, where he was undergoing his initial army training. I was anxious that my own situation didn't make things any more difficult for my parents. It was for that reason that I hadn't told them in detail about what happened to Trish. They had enough on their plate already.

BECAUSE THE BOSS was still ailing, Danny led the way early the next morning, getting us up and on the trolley first thing. We all worked hard with the beaters until we had completed all the work allocated. We arrived back in O'Malley at around two o'clock. The afternoon was spent reading ancient copies of People and Pix magazines borrowed from the dunny. The poorly reproduced photographs of girls in old fashioned swimming costumes were hardly tantalising, but at least they were pictures of the fairer sex. We read the jokes out loud periodically, each of us trying to outdo the other.

Pete did himself proud by frying up a large amount of hot chips to go with his now famous stew. A great discussion ensued that commenced with such lofty topics as the H-bomb and then Australian politics and economics, but it was eventually reduced to soul-searching nostalgia. This was mainly me bemoaning my lost love with Trish. Pete retrieved the situation with some masterly psychiatric techniques. So much so that I was encouraged enough to enjoy a late-night supper of an additional serve of Weet-Bix with sugar and lukewarm water.

THE SNOWMAN still appeared to be unwell the next day (or was he was still drinking?). Danny seemed less than enthused, eventually coming up with the suggestion that we wander up the line checking and tightening any bolts in the line. It was all very confusing. The first days at O'Malley had proved to be really hard graft, and now the work rate was spasmodic at best.

After lunch, I tried to brighten up the day by 'acting the clown' and quoting favourite lines from the Goon Show as well as from Pete and Dud. Being only partially familiar with this strange British humour, my mate pissed himself laughing. Anything to fill in the day!

The evening ended with another tremendous discussion, including heated debates about contraception, the concept of morality and religion. I said that I thought contraception was a great thing – without it, Trish would be looking after our nineteen children, and I'd be slaving away at my office job trying to put enough food on the table.

My God, given half a chance, we could completely fix the world of most of its problems, and all before bedtime.

Our wisdom was truly startling, I chuckled to myself as I fell into a deep slumber.

4

NEW CHUMS

Late one night, a train stopped at O'Malley. We woke up briefly and saw two shadowy figures being ushered into the middle hut by the Snowman.

Early the next day the two new arrivals emerged sleepy-eyed from their cabin. 'G'day guys,' I said as we shook hands. 'My name's Bruce, and this here is Pete. Welcome to O'Malley.'

'Mine's Col,' beamed the tallest of the two. 'This here is Henry, but he's pretty new to Australia, and only speaks a few words of English.'

Just then the Snowman appeared from his cabin bristling with exaggerated vitality and loudly extolling pompous commands.

'Come on you four blokes. No time for gas bagging. That's not the way we get things done around here.'

I gave Pete a wry grin as we made our way to the Ganger's trolley.

'Danny not joining us?' asked Pete.

'No, he's on hygiene duty,' came the reply, causing Pete to shrug in my direction. 'Reckon the Snowman's just impressing the new guys, if you ask me,' he whispered.

The Snowman stopped the trolley a few kilometres down the track, jumped off and proceeded with the same beater training lesson with Henry and Colin that he had applied to us the week before. Once he had us all scraping and belting away to his satisfaction the Snowman wandered off, periodically muttering something about taking important measurements. As usual he didn't pick up a beater again himself for the rest of the day. After we returned to O'Malley in a rather tired state we spotted Danny. 'What have you been up to all day?' asked Pete.

'Oh, just hygiene duty,' replied Danny vaguely.

'Yeah, but what does that actually mean?'

Danny looked around carefully to see that the Snowman was out of earshot.

'Making more Bock beer,' he said in a whisper. 'But don't say I told you.'

'Okay, but what do you brew it in?' I insisted.

'The copper boiler,' said Danny. 'I can make nearly nine gallons in that,' he added with pride.

'What?!' I gawked. 'The same bloody copper we all wash our fucking clothes in?'

'Yeah, but I usually give it a good rinse first.'

'Must be what gives the Bock it's great flavour,' laughed Pete as we wandered slowly back to our cabin.

Col came over to our cabin after dinner with his battery-operated transistor radio. Turned out he was from Tasmania, but we quickly forgave him for that, seeing the precious cargo he had brought with him. The reception faded in and out frustratingly as Col tuned into an Adelaide radio station. We crowded around. We hadn't heard any music for what seemed to be an eternity. We rejoiced to the sound of Paul McCartney's voice singing, 'All You Need is Love.' We all adored The Beatles.

Despite our tiredness from the full days' work, we stayed up late that night glued to that precious little device, and the musical sounds emanating from within, despite the dreadful reception.

FOLLOWING A HARD BUT REWARDING DAYS' work under Danny's direction (the Snowman had 'other' business to attend to – probably bottling the Bock beer), we returned to camp to find a fat envelope full of letters from my family. One very newsy one was from my loving Mum, that was full of a mothers' concern for our wellbeing. She also provided the devastating news that the Olinda Ferny Creek 'Bloods' had lost the first semi-final and wouldn't proceed further in the finals. My guilt about not playing returned in full force.

The other four letters were all from my father. Each affected me greatly. The first was addressed to 'My Dearest Son Bruce'. In it, Dad not only conveyed his pride in me for my 'guts and determination', but also encouraged me to seize the moment so that the experiences gained would serve me well throughout all my life. He said that my relationship with Trish got very serious while we were both so young. It was all a bit much for her parents to take on, but he reassured me that he thought they would eventually come around. I read and reread a couple of lines swallowing hard as I tried to control the lump in my throat.

> *You did nothing wrong son. You just played the game too hard.*
>
> *Both Mum and I are convinced that both you and Peter are going to make us proud, and that nothing but good fortune can come from your bold enterprise.*

The second letter from Dad was addressed 'To Whom it May

Concern' and it stated that I had his full permission to travel interstate to gain experiences and knowledge of Australia, and to seek my future as was my aim.

The third letter was to my mate Pete, wishing him good luck with his ventures, and adding that Bruce could not have a better Cobber to travel with, and advising us to 'take care of each other in everything we do'.

The fourth letter was a reference for Pete, stating that he was an honest, hardworking and studious young man whom he had known for some years. While both Pete and I were several years short of reaching the legal adult age of twenty-one we were both confident of fending for ourselves throughout our travels but having written permission for me to travel from my dad, and a reference for Pete may yet come in handy.

Maybe it was the fact that we had just received our first mail from home, or maybe it was the fact that we suddenly realised the enormity of our actions, but that night Pete and I were both deeply moved by the sincerity expressed in all my parent's letters. We read them over and over in the flickering light of our kerosene lamps.

I missed my brothers and sisters and kept going back to Mum's letter, in which she wrote:

> *The children say they won't forget you, Bruce. They never forget to mention you in their prayers each night.*

We were greeted early the next morning with the news that the only work scheduled for the day for Pete and I was 'joy duty'. What the fuck was that? The Snowman appeared to be hugely enjoying himself as he explained that it consisted of digging a very large hole a long way from the cabins, emptying the contents of the three stinking dunnies into said hole, and filling it in.

'No point in complaining,' I said to Pete as we picked up some shovels. 'I grew up in Belgrave with a dunny at the bottom of the garden until I was 15. Mind you, that one was emptied by the night man once a week.'

We finished the gruesome task in silence except for the occasional grunt, while trying not to breathe in too hard.

We washed our clothes in the copper as usual. I may have been mistaken, but I could swear that I could smell hops as I was hanging them out.

LUNCHTIME CAME and went without the expected Tea and Sugar train arriving.

'Shit,' said Pete. 'We don't have a lot left to eat. I hope it arrives soon.'

Yeah,' I replied. 'And it'll be a dry Saturday night without the beer we ordered too!' Eventually the good old T and S arrived at 8.30 pm. What a blessed sight. A sense of relief enveloped us all as we ran around with barrows in the dark bumping into each other, as we once again played speed shopping.

Our late dinner was followed by another visit from Danny, plus Col with his beloved radio (the still shy Henry stayed in his cabin). We were all in good spirits as we enjoyed a few beers and laughing loudly, when suddenly the Snowman burst in through our cabin door. The abuse levelled at us at high volume was more than a little garbled. All four O'Malley fettlers sat passively staring at the raging bull like figure in front of us. Finishing his tirade the Snowman left our cabin, slamming the door behind him with considerable force.

'Pissed,' said Col.

'In more ways than one,' added Pete.

. . .

Rising late, I revelled in the luxury of Weet-Bix with real milk (God bless the Tea and Sugar). Danny and Col came over for company, but Danny was a bit subdued.

'Everything Okay, Dan?' I asked.

'I have to tell you guys that I'm leaving tomorrow,' said Danny. 'I'm afraid I can't take any more of the old man, so I sent off my resignation last week, and it's been accepted.'

'Aw Danny, we'll miss you big time,' said Pete.

We nodded in agreement.

'Have you told the Snowman; er I mean the Ganger yet?' I asked.

'Only just this morning,' replied Danny.

Just then there was a knock on the door. The Snowman stood there, asking permission to enter. The befuddlement from us was evident on account of the time it took for us to invite him inside.

The Snowman began with a flurry of slurry words (yes, this early in the day) that appeared to be a form of apology. However, his explanation quickly changed to expressions of self-justification. Eventually the Snowman's face turned a vivid purple as he let rip at Danny in particular, calling him a bastard and a pimp. Danny leapt up, shouting and looking as though he were shaping up for a fight. Fortunately though, no fisticuffs ensued. This was altogether too much for Pete and I though. We gave the Snowman a good dressing down. He may be the Ganger and therefore boss of the camp, but he had no right to enter our hut hurling unprovoked abuse. The Snowman retired, still muttering fire and brimstone. A great moral victory for us! Danny stayed, and we shared our stew with him that night (as well as the remainder of our beer).

. . .

NEXT DAY the Snowman took us four fettlers down the track a few kilometres and set us to work tightening bolts with very large spanners. Danny had stayed back at camp. During the lunch break we were sitting around sipping on our billy tea, when a huge goanna appeared from nowhere. It was at least six feet long. I jumped up in alarm.

'Sit down you fool,' shouted the Snowman. 'He may think you're a tree and try to climb up you. See those claws? They'll cut you to ribbons.'

I sat down as the goanna padded away disappearing into the low scrub. 'Were you serious about that goanna?' I asked.

'Out here we call 'em bungarras, and yes, I was bloody serious,' grumbled the Snowman.

'Apart from crows, rabbits and bungarras I haven't seen much wildlife,' I observed.

'No, the roos, dingoes and emus usually stay away from the railway line,' replied the Snowman. They learnt that a long time ago'.

Having a civilised conversation with the boss was proving to be a most unusual experience, but then again, he appeared to be sober for once.

We returned to O'Malley in the afternoon and were just in time to say our farewells to Danny. We grinned at him as he pushed his upper body out through the train window clutching a long-necked Bock beer in his hand. We all stood there waving until the train finally disappeared down the track.

'We've only known Danny for less than a fortnight, but I have to say that I really came to love that guy.'

'Couldn't agree more,' replied Pete, looking despondent.

Col and Henry came over to our cabin after dinner. Our glum mood hadn't improved. Suddenly Col stood up.

'Sod this,' he cried. 'Danny wouldn't want us moping around like this. Let's have a bloody good sing song,' he urged, quickly standing up on a chair and towering over us. Col lifted his gaze towards the roof and began to earnestly sing at the top of his voice. His choice of song was a rousing version of 'Crystal Chandeliers'.

We hadn't seen Col like this before. He sung without a trace of modesty or hesitation. His upright posture, waving arms and fierce expression exuded total defiance and over the top vitality. Pete, Henry and I were all completely transfixed. Charlie Pride eat your heart out. When Col eventually finished, he lowered himself from his perch saying, 'Your turn Bruce.'

Well, being something of a show-off, I wasn't about to be upstaged. Springing up on to my chair I gave a rousing rendition of 'Click go the Shears' with everyone in the room joining in the chorus. Pete followed with Dylan's 'The Times They Are A-Changing', and even Henry hummed us a Hungarian lullaby. The songs continued for what seemed hours. I hadn't had this much fun for ages. Responding to enthusiastic demands from the rest of us Col again gave us an even more strident reprise version of 'Crystal Chandeliers' to finish off the night with all of us joining in with considerable fervour and clapping even louder than before.

EARLY THE NEXT MORNING, we all trooped over to the Ganger's trolley and took up our usual seats on the mechanical device. The Snowman sat, periodically glaring at us, while he attempted to start the petrol driven motor. Not this morning though. The motor refused to cooperate despite the encouragement it was being given by the increasingly fierce demands and explosive rhetoric from the Snowman. Finally, he paused in his endeavours, and grumbled something under his breath.

'What's that he said?' I whispered to Pete.

'I could have sworn he said the word "sabotage"' he whispered back.

Just then the Snowman looked around with venomous eyes.

'Okay, which one of you bastards put sugar in the petrol tank?' he asked.

'I don't think anyone would do that,' ventured Col. 'Let me have a bit of a look at things.' After about ten minutes of Col testing this and that (things mechanical have always been a blank spot for me). Col pressed the starter button, and the little engine roared into life. We were off for another memorable day with the spanners.

We hadn't long finished our evening meal that night when the Snowman burst through the door, again in a state of advanced inebriation.

'Fuckin' shabotage,' he shouted. 'Me trolley's stuffed,' he added, swaying from side to side.

'I think it's okay now boss,' said Pete with admirable restraint. 'It's probably a good idea if you had a bit of a lay down.'

The Ganger stormed back to his cabin.

'Very impressive Pete,' I said, genuinely taken by my mate's composure. 'I shall leave all communication with the boss in your capable hands from now on.'

The rest of the night was spent deep in conversation. Pete and I could always strike up a conversation, but there was something about being out there in the middle of the Nullarbor, in the flickering lamp light, with no other sounds other than the sighing of the wind outside and the crackling of the fire, that stimulated the most animated of discussions.

STRANGE. The next morning, the Snowman emerged on time, sober and in good spirits. 'Go off down the line and bring back as many bolts as you can find and meet me back here in an hour,' he said in a friendly manner.

'What's he up to, I wonder?' said Col.

'Probably just wants more time for breakfast,' replied Pete, as we began meandering along the railway line.

In the hour that we were away we probably found no more than 20 bolts between the four of us, which hardly constituted value for money from the Commonwealth Railways O'Malley labour force. What we could have also picked up (but didn't) would have been about a couple of hundred or so empty bottles and cans that had been unceremoniously dumped from passing trains over the years.

After we returned from our bolt fossicking, the little engine on the trolley started up first go, and all five of us trundled off a short distance up the line, with the Ganger still in high spirits (go figure). After a couple of hours bending our backs with the beaters, we again returned to camp, with the Snowman disappearing into his cabin, without offering further instructions.

We hadn't been back inside our cabin long when Pete let out a howl of anguish.

'I've left the fucking lid off the stew,' he shouted.

Alarmed, I sprinted across the room and peered into the large pot held by my mate. The contents writhed with about a thousand obviously delighted maggots.

'Well mate, you put so much effort into making what was a truly remarkable culinary delight, it wouldn't be right to simply throw it away.'

'You can't eat this,' said Pete dejectedly.

'Hear me out Pete. The famous stew needs a proper funeral, don't you think?'

With that we both trudged outside bearing the still crawling remains in the metal pot. I dug a neat hole outside, and after Pete had tipped the heaving mass into it, we both bowed our heads, while Pete delivered a solemn eulogy. I filled in the hole wondering what the hell we were going to eat for the rest of the week.

I was lounging about lying in the sun while Pete wandered around the camp restlessly. After a time, he appeared in high good humour, bearing a cardboard box. He opened the top, and as I peered into the box, my mate announced, 'Meet our new friends Bruce.'

Inside were two small lizards. They were identical to the dozens we walked over around the camp every day.

'There, there mate,' I said with mock sympathy, patting his arm. 'I'm sure you'll be feeling better soon.'

After waiting impatiently throughout the afternoon, the mail train eventually arrived. To our joy, we received much mail, all of which was read over and over. In particular, my first letter from Trish. She still loved me (sigh)! She said that she was doing mostly okay and was trying to forget that awful night. She missed me every day and was counting down the time until we could be together again. How I wished I could hold her in my arms.

Also included was a letter from a Sassafras resident by the name of Bill Barkley. Pete and I admired him greatly, both as an older friend and a sometime philosopher. The opening few lines struck a real chord:

> I heard that two young mountain lions had cut out for WA. The revelations from your letter were enough to blow my mind, and even my favourite Dylan album jumped a track.

As I read and reread each letter, Pete rustled up some rice and veggies for an unspectacular dinner.

Col came over for a chat afterwards and the conversation turned to religion. The disparity in opinions quickly became more and more obvious. Pete and I had had similar conversations in the past, and usually agreed to disagree on some minor points. He had been brought up solidly in the Catholic faith, and I admitted to being a lapsed Anglican. However, Col's involvement brought a whole new complexity to the whole discourse.

'What faith are you then Col?' asked Pete.

'Jehovah's Witness,' replied Col. 'And very proud of it.'

'Fair enough,' said Pete.

Once we had explored the infallibility of the Pope and the validity of blood transfusions, I begged forgiveness for my extreme tiredness, and wandered off to bed. It was my turn with the sleeping bag, so a night of relative warmth beckoned. I heard the vigorous debate continuing in the next room as I shut my eyes and drifted off into a deep slumber.

JUST AS I had begun to think that the rhythm of work at O'Malley consisted of one hard day followed by several days of general slackness, the Snowman stepped up the pace. Stones on roof, quick breakfast (the last of the bread and jam), and off we went. Beaters yet again, with few breaks. The lack of sustenance was beginning to take its toll.

As we arrived back at camp I said to Pete. 'Listen mate, we have to do something about getting some protein.'

'The Tea and Sugar's due tomorrow,' replied Pete.

'Yeah, but the fucking thing was 8 hours late last week,' I said anxiously. 'What if it's even later this week?'

'Try not to think about it,' shrugged Pete.

'No bloody way,' I persisted. 'I've seen some rabbit traps

under the Snowman's cabin, and I'm going to borrow them so we can catch some bunnies.'

'Righto,' said Pete. 'Where do we set these here traps?' I'd been rabbiting many times with my old mate Alan Bartlett before leaving home, and although we mainly either went shooting or ferreting, I felt that I had a good enough grasp of what was required to secure success. 'Rabbits usually dig their burrows under trees,' I said confidently.

'Trees!' exploded Pete. 'In case you hadn't noticed, we're in the middle of the flamin' Nullarbor. I calmly scanned the horizon, spotting some vegetation way off in a northerly direction. 'This way,' I said with false bravado.

We walked, and then we walked some more. The bloody trees didn't seem to be getting any closer. Eventually we reached a group of about half a dozen stunted bushes standing about five feet high masquerading as trees.

'Now here's a fine Nullarbor forest,' I beamed at Pete.

I began searching for burrow entrances and was quickly rewarded with the sight of at least six tell-tale holes.

'These little buggers may be considered pests by everyone else in Australia,' I enthused. 'But thank God for their resilience, I say.'

We set the traps, bashing the pegs into the ground to secure each one firmly, and popping some of our few remaining bits of carrot on to the foot trap. It was a long walk back to the camp, and the measly feed of rice and eggs that awaited left me hoping quite desperately that the traps would work. I felt permanently hungry and more than a little grumpy.

The arrival of a parcel from my beloved Trish, with her glorious photo and some almost equally glorious tailor-made fags, did cheer me up. She told me again how much she thought of me. Lucky me – this beautiful girl really did love me! Time and distance would be no match for our love.

. . .

THE SNOWMAN LOOKED a bit tired the next morning, saying that after we had completed joy duty, we had the rest of the day off. You beauty!

The hole was dug with alacrity, and the contents of three full dunnies were sloshed into their new earthen home.

We made our way to the Nullarbor forest with a great deal more enthusiasm than we did the day before. Glory be! Of the eight traps we had set, five had rabbits in them. Some were still pulling on their broken legs, trying to escape. I quickly dispatched each rabbit by tightly holding the back of their heads with one hand, and pulling hard on the back legs until I heard their necks break. Quick and clean as possible, although the little buggers continued to kick their legs for some minutes in a final death spasm. We reset the traps and found that the walk back to the camp didn't seem to take as long as before. We ate a whole bunny each for lunch. Fried rabbit never tasted so good.

The friggin' Tea and Sugar was indeed late again, but the pressure was off as we had polished off the three remaining bunnies with a few of our leftover veggies before it arrived. We helped take a new Gangers' trolley off the train, quickly completed our precious shopping and picked up a full dozen long-necked Southwark's from the train's guardsman. The night was spent playing poker (many matches lost by me), followed by a great deal of enthusiastic singing and much drinking of amber fluid. It was a lot easier to have fun on a full stomach.

THE SNOWMAN SUMMONED us early the next morning to help with loading the old Gangers' trolley on to a train that had stopped specially on a Sunday morning at O'Malley. Our thick heads from drinking the night before caused much grumbling, before we eventually returned to bed.

After a late breakfast, we trudged back to the Nullarbor forest to see if yesterday's catch was just a fluke. To our delight, five more rabbits were in the traps. We would be able to share some additional fresh meat with our fellow fettlers, as well as having plenty for ourselves.

The afternoon was starting to drag by when all of a sudden Pete began to quote some poetry for my benefit.

There was movement at the station, for the word had passed around

That the colt from Old Regret had got away

Together we racked our brains to remember the rest of the lines from 'The Man From Snowy River' with a surprisingly high level of recall. Predictably we eventually moved on to 'I Love a Sunburnt Country' but floundered after a few versus.

'We should compose our own poem mate,' I ventured to Pete.

'Absolutely.'

The next three or four hours were given over to composing our great gift to Australian literature.

> Out in the open, where the Mulga grows
> Two lads went a fettlin', the Nullarbor they chose
> Bruce and Pete, their names decried
> Aged twenty-one, or so they lied
> These lads they travelled from Vic to the West
> To see Australia at its colourful best
> Augusta's the place that decided their fate
> 'Cos to eat or not was the heated debate
> So employment they found without further ado
> To a place called O'Malley where people are few
> The Ganger you know called himself Pete
> Whose remarkable pot only equalled his feet
> A grumpy old bastard fully was he

> One night he came over and ruined our tea
> Out on the line from morning till night
> They slaved for the Commonwealth, with all of
>   their might
> Throughout the day the job it was rated
> Those goddam beaters – strewth were they hated
> We were here a few days still learning the ropes
> When along came two more stupid dopes

Eventually we ran out of steam (and beer), conceding that an early night was a good idea.

WE LEFT EARLY on our brand-new trolley, with the Snowman beaming with pride over his new toy. However, even my untrained ear could hear that the motor seemed to be playing up. Regardless, nobody said anything about it, reluctantly getting on with a solid day of scraping and packing with our trusty beaters. We had toughened up considerably since arriving, but the day seemed to go on and on. Eventually the Snowman said enough was enough, so we wheeled the new trolley back on to the tracks.

As we headed back to O'Malley, I could hear the motor missing again, so that the trolley eventually came to a coughing and spluttering stop about a kilometre from camp. The Snowman, Col and Pete all took turns at examining the little motor, without any success in getting her started again. Henry and I sat watching the activity without a great deal of interest, when all of a sudden Henry nudged me violently, and with eyes protruding grotesquely, pointed back down the track.

In the distance was the unmistakable silhouette of a train heading in our direction. 'Guys!' I shouted to the three mechanics hovering over the trolley's motor. 'I don't really want to disturb you, but there is a train coming up our arse at speed.'

Suddenly, as if by magic, the little motor roared into life, and we began the journey back to O'Malley. But, with the motor spluttering still, the little trolley lurched forward uncertainly in fits and starts, as it coughed and spluttered its way towards base camp. I stared back at the approaching train with a feeling of extreme fear enveloping me. It seemed that an ice-cold hand was gripping my heart. I began to plan how I could jump from our faltering, yet still speeding vehicle without horribly maiming myself.

We finally limped into O'Malley with the vision of the approaching train growing larger and larger by the second. There was no time to lose if we were to avoid a catastrophic collision. We were still on the bloody tracks.

'Right,' yelled the Snowman. 'Let's get her off the track.'

We grabbed the turntable with alacrity, and frantically manhandled the trolley onto the siding, with only seconds to spare, before the train roared past us at high speed.

'I'd better replace that magneto tonight,' said the Snowman calmly, as if nothing untoward had happened. I said a little prayer of thanks.

That night after dinner a great sporting event of note took place. Col, Pete and I were still chatting amiably, when all of a sudden Col lifted the cheek of his backside and let rip with an impressive rumble. 'Beat that,' he grinned at us. Not to be outdone, I responded within minutes with an equally admirable effort. Thank heavens Pete had included some beans with dinner, I thought. This could be a serious contest. Col then continued the battle with impressive control, letting out four carefully spaced farts that sounded like someone coughing. Cripes, was there no end to this man's talents. Within minutes I had summoned up sufficient wind to add two more barely audible efforts to my tally. Pete remained flatulently silent. As the night wore on Col continued with infinite control and finesse, and while I continued to be competitive, it was obvious that his lead was unassailable. Despite giving me considerable verbal support, Pete himself appeared completely unable to compete for the entire evening, finally apologising that there appeared to be something wrong with his constitution. Eventually, with the air thick with a most unpleasant and nauseous odour, I conceded defeat. Col proudly departed for home in a jubilant mood, winning by the handsome margin of five seemingly effortless acts of flatus!

THE SNOWMAN PUSHED us hard all day, without bothering to pick up a beater himself as usual. The workers joked with each other throughout the day to break up the boredom. Even Henry attempted some jokes, which we all appreciated, but failed to fully understand. We arrived back at camp to find that a letter had arrived from our old mate Steve Harris.

Pete was preparing the evening meal as I read over Steve's letter.

'What does Steve have to say?' asked Pete.

'Well firstly he's included these,' I said, holding up some pictures of some scantily clad buxom females that had been neatly cut out of a magazine.

'That was rather considerate of him,' said Pete admiring the images from a distance.

'He's also given us a very thorough run down of what he believes are the current sexual tendencies of most of the girls we know back home,' I ventured.

'Do you think he really knows all of those girls though?' quizzed Pete.

'Well, he goes on to say that he spent last Saturday night

with Janet Frobisher in her mum's Austin A30,' I added.

'Shit, that's a very small car to try any sexual shenanigans in,' said Pete with an expression of genuine wonder on his face.

'Yes,' I replied thoughtfully. 'It appears that he had to retire from the field of play with a bad case of cramp.'

'Small wonder,' said Pete as he busied himself with dinner.

'He doesn't say whether Janet was disappointed, or otherwise,' I added. There followed a good minute of silence as we each pondered the situation from the recent Saturday evening event in faraway Sassafras.

'Wasn't it Steve who told us another story about him getting a jar of VapoRub mixed up for a jar of Vaseline?' said Pete suddenly remembering.

'Yep,' I replied. 'Fortunately for the young lady in question, he applied it to himself pre coitus, and not her.'

'Must have taken him quite some time to recover,' proffered Pete.

'Yeah, I don't think consummation was achieved that night either,' I replied. 'That's unusual for Steve. If he is to be believed, he usually has plenty of willing ladies queued up,' quipped Pete.

Later on, Col and Henry came over with a pack of cards. I'd never been particularly good at poker, but after being so badly beaten during the previous nights' contest, I was determined to do better tonight. Lady luck was with me. Poor old Col and Henry left our cabin minus several hundred matches. I then retired to write another letter to Trish.

WE ALL WENT OUT EARLY to work. The day was cool with persistent rain. About mid-morning the Snowman began to look uncomfortable.

'Righto,' he said. 'Let's pack up and head back to camp.' Unusually the noon train slowed and stopped at O'Malley that day, which had all of us walking outside our huts to see why. A small nuggetty bloke jumped off, and the train continued on its journey. Another newbie fettler had arrived. We wandered over to shake his hand, and although obviously pleased with his reception, our new mate clearly only knew a smattering of English words. We only just managed to find out that his name was Quinn before the Snowman arrived and escorted the new recruit to the Ganger's cabin. 'So, the Snowman has another housemate again,' said Col.

'Poor bastard,' agreed Pete.

Wishing to add something constructive to the conversation, I added, 'I reckon that if he's living in with the Snowman, we should give him a nickname too. How about Quinn the Eskimo after the Manfred Mann song?'

'Sounds fair enough,' came the reply from Pete, as we shuffled back to our cabins.

Late that afternoon Pete wandered over to the Gangers' cabin and negotiated the purchase of three bottles of Bock beer. The price was exorbitant, but we all agreed that a night playing cards would be far more pleasant if we had some throat lubricant. Whilst negotiating his purchase, Pete couldn't help but notice the Snowman's huge stash of booze. Apart from the mountain of full Bock beer bottles there were numerous bottles of whisky and flagons of sherry.

Col came over with his famous pack of cards early in the evening, but Henry preferred some solitude. We were just in the process of counting out each players allocation of matches to bet with when Quinn knocked on the door.

'Come on in mate, and join the game,' said Pete.

Quinn was at the table in an instant, his eyes flashing with anticipation. He pulled out his wallet and placed a wad of notes on the table.

'No mate, we play with these,' said Pete showing Quinn the

pile of matches.

Although our new mate could only speak a few words of English, he vigorously let us know that he wanted to gamble with real money.

'Sorry,' said Pete firmly. 'But we don't gamble out here.'

Quinn continued to plead with us by counting out his bank notes and waving them in the air, but we refused to comply. Quinn stood up and disappeared back towards the Snowman's cabin. 'Looks like our new friend has a gambling problem,' said Pete. That's probably why he's come out here. To break the habit.'

'Poor bugger,' said Col, with his Jehovah's sympathy hat on.

WE WERE OUT and about early that morning, in order for the Snowman to impress the newcomer Quinn. After travelling a fair distance on the trolley, we stopped, and the Snowman issued all five of us with our very own crowbar for the day. At last, something different! I was quite surprised how much sideways movement to a railway line can be achieved when five fit blokes prise at it heartily with crowbars.

That night the card game changed to pontoon, with Col, Henry and Pete joining in. Being unfamiliar to the game I opted to watch in order to learn the rules. There was no appearance from Quinn. We all turned in early, each of us complaining about sore muscles from the new work duties. Pete stayed up to write a reply to the letter from his bird.

THE SNOWMAN MUST HAVE HAD a big night. He was waiting impatiently next to the railway line, all red-eyed and squinting. After showering our two cabins with large quantities of rocks, he shouted, 'Where have you blokes been? You're all good for nothing pricks.'

The abuse and insults continued throughout the day as we continued with the same crowbar routine. The tirade slowly abated in line with the Snowman's flagging energy as the day progressed. During lunch, Pete leaned over to me, and in a conspiratorial whisper asked, 'Do you think it's just alcoholism with the boss or do think he's certifiably insane?'

'Both, I should think,' I replied.

After an early dinner, Pete and I began a discussion about National Service and the Vietnam War.

'It's all about stopping Communism,' extolled Pete. 'The French failed to stop the dominoes falling, so the Yanks have stepped up, with our support to get the job done. And of course, your brother's already been called up, added Pete, so you and I should both realise that we could both easily get to go to Vietnam, if we get drafted.'

'Yep,' I replied casually. 'It won't be until 1970 that you and I will have to register, and while I'd prefer not to be called up, if my numbers do come out of the ballot, I'd put up my hand to go to 'Nam for sure.'

'Me too,' said Pete. 'You get paid a lot more by serving overseas.'

'And you get cheap government loans to buy a house when you get back,' I added.

5

MACKA

The day began with a huge responsibility bestowed upon me. Whilst Pete and Col were given menial cleaning tasks, I was to instruct Henry and the Eskimo about the necessary skills to complete the perfect execution of Joy Duty. Afterwards, for some unknown reason, both failed to express their appreciation, which quite baffled me.

As I made my way back to the camp carrying my shit encrusted shovel (it had been a rather messy joy duty due to either the inexperience of my apprentices, or my poor leadership skills) something caught my eye. I was sure that I had seen an animal of some description disappearing around the other side of our cabin. Could be a fox or even a dingo I thought. I took a firm grip of my shitty shovel and carefully made my way to the other side of the cabins. As I rounded the corner, I came face to face with an enquiring canine face, that was dominated by a lop-sided grin and trailing tongue. He was clearly delighted to make my acquaintance, bounding over to me with his large tail wagging furiously. Where the hell had he come from?

'What the fuck are we going to do with a bloody dog?' asked Pete.

'But he's such a handsome and intelligent fella, and he's clearly taken a shine to the best-looking bloke in O'Malley, I replied, so I have no other choice but to adopt him. Anyway, he's got nowhere else to go,' I concluded.

'Shit Bruce,' snapped Pete. 'Just look at him. He's certainly not intelligent, and both of you are far from good looking. The bastard will eat us out of house and home, and what on earth will we do with him when we move on to Perth next week?' I looked over at my admittedly mangy looking new friend, who pricked up his raggedy ears, wagged his moth-eaten tail, and broadened his supercilious grin even further. 'I'll give him half my ration, so the dog stays,' I stated with finality, as I walked over and ruffled his head. 'I've named him MacArthur after the song 'MacArthur Park', but you can call him Macka.'

The Tea and Sugar arrived spot on time allowing us adequate opportunity to buy our provisions and pick up the dozen 75 fluid ounce bottles of Coopers Sparkling Ale we had ordered the week before. A good Saturday night was ensured. After a fine dinner Col and Henry joined us for more games of cards interspersed with much rowdy singing (Crystal Chandelier yet again, to our huge delight).

As the evening wore on too much of the amber fluid flowed. Ignoring the maxim that the most serious and controversial topics should not be brought up when everyone is more than half inebriated, we ploughed on into dangerous territory. 'Blokes shouldn't marry until they're at least 30,' slurred Col, which was strongly supported by Pete.

'Oh yeah,' I yelled back. 'I'll be marrying Trish as soon as I get back to Melbourne.'

'Then you'd be an idiot,' laughed Pete.

I immediately took the bait, and fuelled with too much alcohol, launched myself at Pete, throwing wild punches in his general direction. Henry quickly stood between us, assisted by a swaying Col.

Attempting to gather what remained of my dignity, I blinked at the blurred images before me, turned giddily towards my room, and attempted to say, 'C'mon Macka. It's time for bed.' I'm pretty sure that nothing like those words actually came out of my mouth, yet Macka understood immediately. He accompanied me to my bug-ridden mattress, with his head held high, and without so much as a backward glance at my unsteady protagonists.

I AWOKE LATE the next morning with a dry mouth and huge headache. Thank goodness it was a no work Sunday. Macka was up on the bed snuggled into the back of my legs, surprisingly contented considering the heavy duty yet involuntary farting I had engaged in throughout the night. I got up and tentatively opened the door to the so-called kitchen. Pete was up, had started the fire and the kettle was already boiling. Apart from that, he looked as bad as I felt. 'Sorry about last night,' I ventured cautiously. 'Nah, it was my fault,' said Pete. 'Let's have some breakfast and a mug of tea.' Macka bounded out of the bedroom at the mention of food.

The day drifted on. Our listlessness was aggravated by the huge hangovers we had inflicted upon ourselves. We dragged ourselves out to the Nullarbor forest with Macka trotting along beside us. As we neared the stunted bushes, Pete said, 'You had better restrain that mutt of yours, otherwise he'll eat our entire catch.'

Another good bounty of bunnies was had, so the food situation would be sufficient, even though we had another mouth to feed.

It was clear that O'Malley was becoming a bit too isolated for us. We were bored and needed some nightlife – not to mention some female company. Thank goodness we had passed in our notice to leave O'Malley in a week's time.

When we walked down towards the trolley the following morning, the Snowman emerged from his cabin, dressed only in his undies. What a sight that was.

'Too tired,' was all he said, as he disappeared back inside.

It was a fine morning, so Pete and I stripped down to our shorts, and lazed in the sun. Macka was delighted to have our company, dropping odd bits of refuse on to various parts of our bodies, and then standing back grinning, and waiting expectantly for signs of appreciation.

Long after lunch, the Snowman reappeared looking a bit sheepish. After locking Macka inside our cabin, we all piled onto the trolley and took off. Every now and then we would stop, and the Snowman would direct either Pete or myself to shin up a telegraph pole to remove a crows' nest or two. After a while it became evident that this would be the only work for the day. No problem for us. We both prided ourselves on our climbing ability. At the top of one pole, finding yet another crow's nest, I found a newly laid egg. The newcomers hadn't seen the old 'catch the egg' trick, I thought to myself, so I picked up the egg, and threw it down to Col, yelling 'catch it'. He saw it coming, neatly stepped back, and let it smash into pieces at his feet. 'I wasn't going to fall for that old trick,' smiled Col. I guess that proved that I was the only really gullible fettler out there that day.

We returned to camp to find a newsy letter from my Mum about the 'comings and goings' at home. She sounded happy for me too:

Dad and I are so pleased to know that you are settling down fine, and that the calm there in O'Malley is doing you good, both mentally and physically.

Hope you are keeping a diary. This'll make good reading in a few years' time.

Love Mum

P.S. Often think of you

It was such a delight to receive her wonderful caring letters, although it did seem that my attempts to reassure her about my wellbeing had been overly successful. The only unsettling matter that night was the glowing dog turd I found on the bedroom floor. Still, the night was so cold, that I found it easy to forgive my newly found canine mate, as he once again snuggled into the back of my legs, at least keeping that part of me warm.

IT WAS straight into beater work in the morning, and as the sun rose in the sky we began to perspire profusely. Both Pete and I stripped down to our shorts, whilst Quinn and Henry also began peeling off layers of clothing. As usual Col kept his long trousers and thick lumberjack style shirt on throughout the early morning. Eventually, about an hour before the lunch break, Col couldn't stand the heat any longer, and stripped off his thick shirt. The rest of us stopped work immediately, blinded by the reflected light. Col's skin was almost alabaster white. 'Cripes,' said Pete. 'There's a torso that's never seen the sun before.'

'Leave off,' snorted Col, as he belted more rocks under the sleepers with great ferocity. The rest of us gracelessly chuckled even louder.

The walk to the Nullarbor Forest, accompanied by our leaping canine buddy was a delight in the fading light of the day. We were rewarded with the largest rabbit yet. The return walk to O'Malley was completed with much laughter, as Pete and I took turns throwing an old stick off into the flat wilderness and watching Macka bound after it.

Once I had skinned and gutted our largest rabbit, Pete cooked it up efficiently in the frying pan with some onions and peas. It was quite a meal.

THE NEXT DAY was Col's birthday, so were in good spirits. The Snowman stayed at the camp, designating Pete to the position of Ganger for the day. The day before I had purchased three bottles of Bock beer from the Snowman, so we were looking forward to a toast to our friend in style that evening.

We returned to find that more mail had arrived. Included was a much-anticipated letter from Trish, several letters from Pete's family, and a large parcel from Mum. The parcel contained some articles of clothing, a large bag of lollies (a previously unheard-of luxury on the Nullarbor), and my cherished Yashica 35mm camera, as requested. I had taken up photography as a hobby earlier in the year, encouraged and mentored by my Uncle Jim, who then worked as police officer in Victorian Police Forensic Department. He had given me a great deal of very useful advice, so my photographic skills were improving considerably. 'Let's take some shots of O'Malley before we leave next Sunday,' enthused Pete. Our disappointment was palpable when I discovered that no film had been included with my camera.

I also had a letter from my mate Mick Roitman. It was a newsy affair, but it was the final PS at the end that took my eye:

If you had dropped by before you left, I would have given you some cash. Tell me next time!

He was being completely genuine, and I appreciated the gesture greatly

Col came over to our cabin, so I went to fetch our celebratory bottles of grog. Alas, they were nowhere in sight. 'Someone's swiped the booze,' I yelled in anger. Col and Pete stomped over.

'Well, the Eskimo and Henry have been with us all day, and in any case, they barely drink,' stormed Pete.

'So, who does that leave?' said Col furiously.

I knocked hard at the Gangers hut door, but nobody opened it. 'You're nothing but a stingy old prick,' I bellowed venomously in the general direction of the Snowman's residence. There was still no reaction, so I trudged slowly back to our cabin, opened my package from home, and offered Pete and Col each a hard-boiled lolly as a poor substitute for Col's now subdued birthday celebration.

THE NEXT MORNING the Snowman acted as if nothing had happened. He obviously realised that Pete and I only had a couple of days of work left, before we would be on our way, looked from his demeanour, like he was going to push us hard. We locked Macka in a back shed before leaving, locking the heavy door. The mutt barked his disapproval as we made our way to the trolley.

We must have been at least 10 miles down the line before we stopped and began some heavy labouring work. Sometime later, as I was belting some more rocks into submission, I heard some heavy panting close behind me. Thinking it might be our boss sneaking up on me (I believed anything strange was possible from him by now), I turned quickly to see Macka's grinning mush, with his tongue hanging from his mouth, and dripping with saliva as usual. He must have escaped and run the whole bloody ten miles. Boy what a stubborn, dedicated, and dumb dog. He rested for most of the remainder of the day and appeared to enjoy the return trolley ride home immensely, seated between my legs, with his big ears flapping wildly in the strong wind.

After we had arrived back at camp, we heard Henry yabbering loudly from the other side of his cabin. This being extremely unusual behaviour from our normally taciturn mate, we rushed over to see what the commotion was about. We arrived to find Henry cradling a very young bunny in his hands. He'd found it nibbling on some potato peelings, and quickly picked it up. 'Good job Macka didn't find it first,' I ventured.

'He's lucky that he's so small, or I'd have him in my frying pan by now,' added Pete.

Henry paid no attention to us as he fussed around with a cardboard box making the wee animal as comfortable as possible.

THE NEXT DAY was to be our last working day at O'Malley, and it began with instructions from the Ganger to go off 'bolt fossicking' again. What a fruitless exercise it turned out to be. Merely another excuse for the Snowman to do bugger-all. At least it provided Macka with some company as he sniffed and padded his way along the side of the railway track. At one point I picked up a useful looking piece of timber.

'This would make an ideal cricket bat,' I said.

'Oh yeah,' replied Pete. 'In case you hadn't noticed, we don't have a bloody ball.'

'Here, take it,' I insisted.

I picked up an empty steel beer can and bowled in Pete's direction. In no time at all we were both engaged in a fun game of cricket with our improvised equipment. The act of bashing the hell out of empty flying beer cans felt strangely cathartic.

Eventually we were called back to camp to begin some work. This time we plonked our furry buddy into the laundry, carefully locking all windows and the door. Off we went on the trolley for what we expected to be our last time, eventually stopping about five or six miles down the line.

I kept an eye open for Macka, and sure enough, about an hour after we arrived at our designated workplace, I spotted the unmistakable sight of our mutt mate bounding towards us in the distance.

'How in heavens name did he get out of that locked laundry?' said Pete. 'We should have named him Harry bloody Houdini'.

The Snowman kept us working well past clock off time, seeming to take real pleasure in taunting us while he still could.

It came as no surprise on our last day that the Snowman ordered us to take on 'joy duty' the next morning. But we started fuming when he insisted that, after completion of this odious exercise, we were all to get back on the trolley for some additional heavy duty packing with beaters. The bastard was obviously intent on making our life a misery until the very end of our stay. We made it back to camp just in time for the arrival of the Tea and Sugar. We obviously didn't need to buy many provisions, but picked up our case of beer from the train guard. We planned to make our last night in O'Malley a memorable one.

The Snowman approached us, saying that our final pay packet would be available at Parkeston Railway Station near Kalgoorlie, when we arrived there. Both Pete and I looked sceptically at the Ganger.

'How do we know we can trust you?' asked Pete.

'I guess you have no choice,' came the reply, as our boss strolled nonchalantly back to his cabin.

We had a hearty meal with the food we'd just bought and washed it down with some good Coopers beer. Col, Henry, and the Eskimo all came over to our cabin, and quickly joined in the merriment. The singing was loud and unrestrained from our well lubricated throats, and the jokes became more and more bawdy, as the night wore on.

Suddenly the Snowman burst into our cabin, swaying, obnoxious and full of unabated anger. His face was contorted with a furious rage. The Boss's huge fists clenched and unclenched, as he gave little skips of annoyance.

'Piss off you prick,' I said, walking up to the angry figure before me.

I should have seen it coming. The Snowman's first haymaker hit me flush on the jaw with the full force of an arm and fist that had both been conditioned by thirty odd years of swinging a beater. My vision exploded into shooting stars, as I reeled from the blow. I only just regained sufficient vision to see the second vicious blow coming, but it was just enough time for me to sway sideways, so that his fist missed me, but only just. I shook my head, trying to clear my vision, while I danced around him. He came at me again, with his arms swinging wildly. This time I caught him with a sold left-hand jolt to the bridge of his nose, and quickly followed up with a hard right hand to the side of his head. The Snowman stopped in his tracks, shook his head, and came after me again.

Bloody hell, I thought to myself. Those two blows would have stopped most blokes.

As the Ganger lunged forward, I sidestepped, causing him to unbalance. As he tried to right himself, I let go a flurry of well-aimed strikes to his body and followed up with two more heavy blows to his face. The Snowman's arms fell to his side, as the expression on his face suddenly began to look rather strange and stupefied. I grabbed him by the front of his shirt and half threw, half pushed our erstwhile boss through the fly wire door. It came off at the hinges, and partially cushioned his body as he landed flat on his back outside. 'And don't come back,' I roared, with the adrenaline surging strongly through my veins.

The Snowman crawled away into the night as my fellow fettlers clapped and cheered, thrusting a bottle of beer into my hand. In keeping with the old bush rules of one on one only in a fight, my colleagues had not intervened, but were clearly delighted with the end result. The singing resumed, this time with lots of jigging and dancing. There was no doubt about it. Blokes still enjoyed watching a good stoush, particularly if their favourite wins.

After about an hour, I began to wonder what condition the Snowman was actually in. 'Who cares,' Pete shouted. 'The bastard got just what he deserved.'

I wasn't so sure, and slipped out quietly, making my way to the Gangers cabin. I knocked loudly on his door, which opened almost immediately with the Snowman's full figure filling the space. To my surprise, he grinned at me and thrust a near full bottle of Bock beer into my hand. 'Where'd you learn to fight like that?' he asked, full of what appeared to be unrestrained admiration.

'Well, I'll be,' I thought.

I eventually returned to our cabin more than an hour later,

very pissed indeed. 'Where the bloody hell have you been?' slurred Pete. 'Oh, just had a few beers with the Snowman,' I just managed to say, as I lurched towards my bedroom with the ever-loyal Macka following me.

PETE and I rose with very sore heads around mid-morning. My pounding cranium made worse by a very tender jaw from the one blow the Snowman had landed at the start of our fight. 'You really cleaned up the boss last night,' said Pete. 'Shit mate,' I responded. 'If he had got just one more punch in, I would have been mincemeat.'

'Yeah maybe,' said Pete. 'But what happened when you went over to his cabin? You were over there for ages.'

'Well, he was still off his face, but still coherent enough to be very complimentary,' I replied. 'I think we just talked crap after that,' I added.

'Bloody amazing,' concluded Pete, shaking his head.

Our train was scheduled to arrive in O'Malley at 11.30 that morning, so we quickly finished our tidying up and packed our few possessions. At just after 11 we sauntered over to Col and Henry's cabin. Quinn the Eskimo was there as well. 'The boss not well,' said Quinn, adding. 'He not wishing to see you.'

'Fair enough,' I said. Just then Pete let out a howl.

'Shit Bruce, I can hear the bloody train coming. It's fucking early for once.'

We rushed outside to indeed see our train approaching O'Malley, and fast. I quickly tied a rope around Macka's neck, whilst Pete took our bags over to where we expected the train to stop. All five of us were rushing up to each other embracing and frantically saying our farewells as the train finally stopped. I got on board with Macka, and Pete threw me our bags. The guard's whistle sounded as we both poked out our heads from the windows to wave to our mates for the last time. As we did so, a portly figure limped out from the Gangers hut wearing dark glasses. The Snowman struggled over to the railway line as the train began to gather speed, waved, and yelled something that was carried away on the wind. We waved back at the four figures, who all stayed by the track with arms raised until we could see them no more.

'Now,' said Pete. 'We've got one station between us and Cook. It's time to make a decision about Macka. I know we couldn't leave him at O'Malley. The bloody Snowman would probably have eaten him eventually.'

'Do you think he was that insane?' I asked.

'Yep, I most certainly do,' confirmed Pete. 'But the fact still remains that we can't take Macka to Perth with us mate.'

I sat stewing on Pete's statement. Suddenly we passed through Fisher. I knew that the next stop was going to be Cook and it was the only township with a reasonable number of people living there. Every other station between Cook and Kalgoorlie would be nothing more than small fettlers camps. Our only option was to let our canine buddy out at Cook.

As the train moved towards that small town, situated smack in the middle of the Nullarbor, Macka sat on his seat, grinning at me in his usual manner. The crazy stupid mutt had grown on me more than I wanted to admit, but I knew I had to make a tough decision, for his sake as well as ours. The train eventually came to a screeching stop. I gave Macka a final ruffle of his tousled head and waited for the whistle. Once I heard it, Pete opened the door, and slipping off Macka's rope, I pushed him out the door. As the train gathered speed, I looked out of the open window to see Macka standing forlornly looking back at us. Then suddenly I could have sworn I saw him shrug. He then turned around, and padded away from the train tracks, heading towards the Cook township. 'I'm sure he'll soon find another sucker to look after him,' said Pete.

'I hope so,' I said, feeling like I was the biggest prick in the world. I was starting the long journey to Kalgoorlie and on to Perth with a very heavy heart.

6

GO WEST YOUNG MAN

After a long, cold night on the slow-moving train, we eventually arrived at Parkeston on the outskirts of Kalgoorlie. We leapt off and went straight to the Commonwealth Railways pay office. A good deal of our pay had been held back until we finished our tenure as fettlers, so we expected a fair lump of dough. The Paymaster looked coldly at us, saying that our pay hadn't been made up yet, and to come back at 2pm.

Thoroughly pissed off, we took a cab into Kalgoorlie to kill some time. We knew that Kal was a large and rough miner's town in the bush but found it to be a less than inspiring conglomerate of ramshackle old buildings.

We'd been cooped up in O'Malley, with only four other blokes to socialise with so had been hoping to find some civilized company. No such luck. Not at this time of the morning anyway. We killed some time by lodging our bags at the Kalgoorlie ticket office and buying a train ticket to Perth for the trip scheduled to leave that night. We then poked around some nondescript shops, serviced largely by disinterested shopkeepers, finally grabbing a barely passable hamburger from a greasy fish and chip shop, before we took a cab back to Parkeston.

We walked up to the Pay Office at the appointed hour of 2 pm, only to be told to come back in an hour.

'Fucking bureaucracy,' raged Pete. 'We've bloody well slaved for these bastards, in the middle of nowhere for weeks, all the time being subjected to the direction of a raving lunatic, and the pricks can't even have our pay ready on time.'

'Yes, but at least they gave us free transport out of there, Pete.'

Finally, at 3 pm we received our pay packets and quickly added up the money from them, together with the dough we already had in our wallets. 'Shit,' I said excitedly. I've got a total of $160.'

'Me too,' said Pete punching the air. 'It's an absolute fortune.'

We jumped back into another cab and headed back to Kal.

'I vote we have a pot in every fuckin' pub,' I said.

'Yeah, let's have a bloody good pub crawl.'

We rolled into the first hotel we came to, and after having two full pots of Hannan's draught beer plonked on the bar in front of us, Pete asked the barman, 'How many pubs are there in Kal?'

'About 30-odd I guess,' came the casual reply.

After pausing for a minute or so, Pete then asked, 'How many in the main street then?'

'There's exactly eleven,' came the reply.

'I reckon we might modify our target to just the pubs in the main drag.'

'And maybe have a glass in each, rather than a pot.'

It was in the ninth pub that Pete leaned over to me, and obviously in a moment of beer-induced good cheer, said, 'You know, if it hadn't been for you, we wouldn't be off on this great adventure,' and after a brief pause, he added, 'I think you're a bloody genius.'

'There's some facts you can't argue with,' I joked.

It was in the eleventh pub that the barman said. 'Listen fella's, you both look as though you might have had enough beer for the time being'.

'But we've still got almost two hours to kill before the train leaves for Perth,' Pete slurred.

'Well why don't the two of you pop up to Hay Street and amuse yourselves for an hour or so?' replied our friendly barman.

'What's in Hay Street?' I asked with genuine innocence.

'Girls,' he grinned. 'There are no legal brothels in Australia, but in Kal, they're tolerated by the authorities.

HAY STREET, or at least the part of it that our taxi driver delivered us to, consisted of a long row of small shed like structures, each with a small veranda out the front, close to the road. Seated in some of the verandas was a woman, either reading or knitting.

Despite our relatively half inebriated state, Pete and I suddenly felt a bit nervous.

'Hello,' smiled a plain looking middle-aged woman blinking through her thick spectacles. 'Are you boys looking for some company?'

'Well, yes,' I stammered.

'You've come to the right place then. My friend Joan and I are free right now.'

'How much is it then?' said Pete cautiously.

'It's ten dollars if we strip naked, or six if we just lift up our dress,' said one of the women in a matter-of-fact tone.

I nodded to Pete as I opened the veranda gate in front of me and made my way to where the bespeckled woman waited.

Inside the shed, it was quite dark, but I could just make out a stout timber bed in the corner that was covered by a clean starched sheet.

'Let's have a look at your manhood then', said my female companion. She appeared in front of me holding a kidney shaped bowl that contained a green looking fluid that smelt strongly of disinfectant. As I opened my fly, she expertly took out my pecker, gently placed it into the bowl, and washed it with some cotton wool. She then took my hand and walked me towards the bed.

'Is it going to be the six- or ten-dollar version, love?' she asked me.

In for a penny, I thought, handing her a brand new ten-dollar bill.

Sadly, the physical isolation I'd endured over several weeks on the Nullarbor proved fatal to my performance. My visit was over in no time at all. My faded courtesan smiled fleetingly, before turning back to her book.

I stood on the other side of the road as I waited for Pete to emerge from Joan's boudoir. I heard angry voices emanating from within. Eventually Pete reappeared, red faced and obviously very agitated. He stormed across the road, muttering expletives.

'What happened mate?' I asked, as we made our way back down Hay Street.

Pete paused, and then said, 'I thought I'd just go for the six dollar job, but then I couldn't get a bloody hard-on and the damn woman refused to give me my money back.'

I put my hand reassuringly on Pete's shoulder and said, 'Well mate, at least you got a professional knob wash.'

'Fucking expensive bit of hygiene.'

'Shouldn't have been so stingy.'

WE HEADED off for a counter meal at a pub around the corner from the railway station. Although basic fare, it was nice to sit down to a meal with other people around us.

'The train leaves in 15 minutes,' said Pete as we finished our dinner. 'I'll go and get some grog for the journey, if you get the bags?'

'See you on the train,' I agreed.

Pete sat down in the train carriage, puffing a bit after carrying the full case of Hannan's beer. He placed it carefully on the carriage floor and pulled out a half bottle of Johnnie Walker scotch whisky from his pocket, placing it on a wall bottle holder.

'Just a backup if we need it,' he explained.

Unlike many of the trains on the Nullarbor, the Perth Express commenced its journey precisely on time at 7pm.

Pete and I were swigging straight from a bottle of bitter each when a sailor joined us. He introduced himself as Phil from Wellington in New Zealand.

'You're a long way from the sea, mate,' I said.

He gave Pete a couple of coins, ignored me, and opened a bottle for himself. Within 20 minutes three or four other thirsty travellers had joined the session. Our voices became louder and louder, and eventually the singing started. Pete was in particularly fine voice, giving a spirited version of Presley's 'Return to Sender', complete with a full hip swinging impersonation of the great man.

The growing crowd of well-oiled travellers around us heartily joined in the chorus, clapping and stomping in appreciation. I followed with a shaky rendition of 'Women' by the Easybeats.

My Stevie Wright impersonation was probably quite pathetic, but our newly found mates gave me great encouragement, nonetheless. By now the party was in full swing, with everyone joining in and singing increasingly raucous versions of their favourite songs. From our increasingly drunken perspective, the highlight of the night was when Pete and I rose to our feet and gave lusty voice to Col's unique version of Crystal Chandeliers, complete with his ridiculously strenuous hand gestures. He would have been most proud, had he been there.

Eventually, the train guard entered our carriage, saying that if we didn't quieten down, we would all be forcibly removed. He received a loud Bronx cheer for his efforts, before returning to his end of the train, shaking his head.

'I'll be glad when I've had enough,' I slurred to the Kiwi sailor as we both swayed in and out of time with the movement of the clattering carriage. He nodded in agreement, his face resplendent with a ruddy grin.

Eventually the beer started to run out, and our companions lurched their way back to their carriages. It was just as well: I couldn't possibly have drunk another ounce.

'This really is a great train trip,' I thought to myself, as I drifted into unconsciousness.

MY HEAD ACHED and my mouth felt like it was coated with fur as I awoke into a semiconscious state. We were entering the suburbs of Perth, so I brightened myself up. After all, this was our grand destination. Pete was obviously in a similar state of health, but he too perked up, as we both stared out the windows, immediately impressed with what we were seeing.

We arrived at 8am at the main station in Perth and found a

helpful accommodation guide board without difficulty. Quickly dismissing the list of posh hotels, we found some interesting sounding nearby boarding houses. After swallowing a bacon and egg sandwich from the railway café and gaining our bearings from a newly purchased map of Perth, we made our way to the first boarding house address.

An hour later I looked at Pete. 'Strewth, what a disgusting array of doss houses,' I moaned. 'I wouldn't allow my worst enemy to stay in any of those dumps'.

'I think we might have to go a bit up market,' agreed Pete. 'I noticed a residential hotel by the name of the Derward in Murray Street, not far from the Perth Town Hall. Let's check it out.'

We stood out the front of a large, old fashioned brick hotel. The sign identified it as purely residential, with no bars or restaurant. Inside it was clean and the tariff moderate, so we booked a room with two single beds. The opportunity to luxuriate in a long hot shower, followed by a shave, was glorious to say the least.

As we were leaving our new temporary home to take in the city sights, I noticed a sign near the exit with words to the effect that all doors to the establishment closed at midnight sharp, and they would not reopen again until 6 am the next morning.

'Better not get home too late Pete,' I said. 'That sign appears unequivocal'.

Pete just shrugged as we headed off to the nearby Wentworth Hotel for a slap-up counter lunch. We had money in our pockets, and we were starving.

We wandered around Perth, getting our bearings. I found a photographic shop and purchased a roll of Ilford HP4 35mm black and white negative film.

'At last, we can start recording some images of our trip,' I said. 'I would have given a lot to have taken a few photos of

O'Malley. Who knows when we will get an opportunity to see that place again'.

We paused outside a Perth Cinema.

'This movie looks interesting, and it starts in ten minutes,' I said looking at a poster for the latest saucy French romp 'Benjamin'.

'Let's go in then,' replied Pete.

The movie was set in seventeenth century France with the main storyline consisting of a scrawny 17 year old male being unrealistically pursued by a number of very attractive women in various states of undress. To our frustration, he seemed not to know what to do when they caught up with him.

'Well at least we got to see Katherine Deneuve's boobs,' said Pete after we left the theatre.

'Probably worth the price of admission in their own right,' I agreed. 'The rest of the movie didn't make a lot of sense though'.

We dined at the George Hotel in St Georges Terrace, which was a good deal more upmarket than the Wentworth. Both of us had voracious appetites that had no doubt developed from the frugal eating forced upon us whilst toiling on the Nullarbor. Afterwards, still looking for some mid-week action, we found our way to The Savoy Hotel, but quickly saw that the only real entertainment there was courtesy of a very drunken sailor. We asked the barman where we might hear some live music.

'Oh, the best place during the week is Pinocchio's Night Club in Murray Street,' he said. 'They open about 10 pm, but it's BYO, so take a few bottles with you from the bottle shop'.

Pinocchio's was indeed quite a lavish affair, and already jumping to a Four Seasons cover band, who were providing creditable versions of the do-wop band's big hits. As we arrived the lead singer raised his falsetto voice to such extraordinary heights that it left both of us concerned as to the authenticity of his testicular accoutrements.

Pete and I sat down, took the tops off a couple of bottles of Emu Bitter, and looked at the couples dancing on the floor. It looked like fun.

Helen and Margaret were two charming ladies somewhere in their twenties. They enthusiastically accepted our offers to dance as soon as Pete and I approached their table. I smiled at Helen warmly as we grooved to a spirited version of *'Walk Like a Man'*, only sitting down when the band took a short break. Both she and Margaret were happy enough to share a glass of beer with us but made it abundantly clear that they usually preferred wine with bubbles in it.

'Classy chicks,' I thought approvingly.

The conversation flowed throughout the night, except for when we were throwing ourselves about the dance floor with unrestrained abandon. Both girls appeared to be fascinated to learn about the adventure we were engaged in, eagerly wanting to know more about the next steps in our plans. Eventually I glanced at my watch and sat bolt upright. It was 11.50 pm. Ten minutes to lock out time.

Our reaction was embarrassingly Cinderella-like, but unlike her, we were able to quickly arrange to meet both girls in the morning. 'We'll pick you both up from the Derward in my car at 11 tomorrow morning, and show you around Perth,' said Helen, as Pete and I headed for the exit, throwing air kisses back at the girls. We made it through the front doors of the Derward with seconds to spare.

We lay on our beds and chatted for quite some time about our eventful day, particularly our luck in meeting our two extremely charming new female acquaintances.

'They're pretty good looking and both have cars,' I enthused. 'I think we could have a pretty good time with these girls.'

'Steady on there, Bruce,' said my ever-cautious mate. 'Helen may just be more interested in the wad in your wallet, than the wad in your jocks,' he said with a laugh.

'No, the simple fact is that she has already fallen for my dazzling charm,' I replied confidently, pulling the blankets up to my chin.

After a brief silence, Pete looked over in my direction.

'What the devil are you grinning at now?' he asked.

With my eyes already closed I mumbled, 'I'm just finishing the night dreaming about Catherine Deneuve's wonderful assets.'

'I assume you to mean her acting skills?' enquired Pete.

'Yes, both of them,' I joked back, as I drifted off to sleep.

WE AROSE at the leisurely hour of eight o clock, showered, and popped across the road to a nice little café for tea and toast. We were back at the Derward foyer right on time at 11 and waited for the girls to show up.

They arrived about 40 minutes late but looking even better than they had the night before.

'Let's start the day with a drink,' suggested Pete.

'Ooh yes,' smiled Margaret. 'Why don't we go to the Palace Cocktail Bar?'

The Palace was a pretty swish affair with an ever so gracious waitress. The girls soon had two sugar-coated brandy crusta filled glasses before them and doing their best to show us that these were entirely familiar surroundings for them both. Equally keen to impress, Pete and I each had a flaming glass of Galliano.

Although superficial, the chat was warm and friendly, so we ordered a second round, and continued the session.

'There's a terrific restaurant at Kings Park,' said Margaret. 'We could go there for lunch'.

'Good idea,' said Pete, calling for the bill. I could have sworn there was a fleeting look of incredulity on Pete's face, before he quickly regained his composure, and paid the bill with superb aplomb.

That was probably a few days' worth of swinging a beater, I thought quietly.

Kings Park was a beautiful botanical park on an elevated headland with sweeping views over the Swan River to the Perth CBD. The four of us strolled through stunning parkland, only to find that the restaurant was fully booked.

'Never mind,' said Helen brightly. 'It's only a half an hour drive to Fremantle, which we would love to show you'.

'Lunch there then,' I agreed.

The drive south was indeed pleasant with Helen driving, me sitting happily beside her, with Pete and Margaret cosily cramped together in the back seat of the small Hillman Minx.

'Fremantle is a port city with a wonderful atmosphere', said Margaret.

Her voice was rather posh, I thought.

'Isn't there a bloody big prison there too?' asked Pete.

'Yes, we don't know much about that', responded Marg quickly, effectively shutting down any further conversation about such a distasteful topic.

We dined at a renovated pub named the Beaconsfield and washed the exquisite meal down with several bottles of Mateus Rose, carefully chosen with flair by Pete (he really was excelling himself). The girls were by now becoming quite flirtatious, which was fine by us. We strolled around Victoria Quay admiring the new Fremantle Passenger Terminal and holding hands.

As we drove back to Perth, Pete asked our ever-attentive acquaintances whether they would like to have dinner with us the following evening. Both girls readily agreed, suggesting that the Adelphi Hotel on St George's Terrace would be a great place to meet and dine.

'We could go on to the Top Hat nightclub afterwards,' suggested Helen.

'Excellent idea,' I enthused. 'Shall we meet at 7.30?'

Later that night, I sat at a small desk in our room, penning a letter to Trish. Was I feeling guilty about my flirtatious afternoon with Helen? A little. It was no use talking to Pete about my conflicted feelings – he was already snoring away in bed.

A FLASHY MENSWEAR store beckoned us the next morning, so Pete bought some new fashionable strides, while I found a great button down collared blue shirt. We took photos of ourselves for posterity, and after lunch began the search for some less expensive digs. This proved spectacularly unsuccessful, but both Pete and I were so focused on meeting our sexy new female friends, we didn't worry about it very much at all.

The Adelphi proved itself to be the finest of the dining residences we had so far experienced in Perth, which was no mean feat. All the others had been very much up market. We all ordered filet mignon steak, with Pete again rising to the occasion by ordering a bottle of chilled Cold Duck sparkling red wine (such refinement). As we left the Adelphi, it was evident that the girls had each come in their own cars, so we separated into couples, as we drove on to the Top Hat.

We entered the portals of the nightclub red cheeked and giggling. After half an hour of upbeat pop songs, the five-piece band, brought some refinement to the evening by surprisingly singing some slow burn ballads very well, starting with a cover version of The Union Gap's 'Young Girl'. Helen snuggled up close in my arms, as we slowly moved around the dance floor.

'Let's go for a drive,' she whispered huskily in my ear. After briefly explaining the situation to Pete, and receiving an enthusiastic thumbs up in return, Helen and I were out of the nightclub door, and into her Hillman with a speed that would almost have appeared as unseemly haste to anyone else that may have been paying attention.

We entered the Kings Park precinct and Helen parked discretely away from the bright street lights. I'd like to say I was instantly taken by the fantastic evening view of Perth in the distance, but I was immediately otherwise engaged. Boy oh boy, the promise that I had seen in Helen was really being realised, and then some. Her kisses were full and passionate as the car radio played 'Different Drum', sung by the Stone Pony's.

Our enthusiasm was gaining momentum when the DJ casually gave the time check.

'It's 11.45 folks,' the DJ said. 'For those getting up early tomorrow for work, you had better be heading off to your beds.'

'Oh Helen,' I moaned. 'Unless we have somewhere else to go for the evening, I have to be back at the Derward before midnight, otherwise I'll be locked out'.

'Bugger,' Helen said. 'I still live at home with Mum and Dad, so we can't go there'.

We drove back in silence, feeling as though we hadn't finished something important. We pulled up outside the Derward at 11.58, and just had time for one more warm embrace and kiss, before I sprinted through the hotel door, with seconds to spare for a second time. Fuck it! So close, and yet so far!

I wandered up the stairs to our second-floor bedroom. Opening the door, I said in a loud voice, 'How did you get on mate?'

Silence followed. 'Shit,' I muttered.

Obviously, Pete and Margaret had had somewhere to go back to. I kicked an imaginary cat before getting into bed and thinking about how Pete and Margaret were probably tucked up in bed somewhere, shagging each other stupid.

THERE WAS a loud knock on the door. I woke up and looked at my watch. It was precisely one minute past 6 am. I staggered over to the door, opened it, and was astonished to see my bleary eyed and somewhat rumpled mate, blinking at me.

'What happened to you?' I asked.

Pete stomped into the room. 'Margaret got me back a couple of minutes after the damned bewitching hour,' he said with considerable force. 'I bashed on the doors, but no bastard would unlock them'.

'So, what did you do?' I said, trying to sound compassionate.

'I went round the back of the hotel and tried to shin up a drainpipe to an open bathroom window,' he said with pure venom in his voice. 'I actually made it as far as halfway up,' he added. 'Strewth Pete,' I said. 'That window would be 40 foot off the ground'.

'Yes,' he replied. 'I very nearly fell, so I eventually gave up and found a boat in that shed out the back,' he added, pointing to a large old iron storage shed through our bedroom window. 'I crawled under a tarpaulin that was covering the boat. Why the fuck didn't you come looking for me?'

'There was no bloody point in both of us being locked out,' I reasoned. 'And in any case, I thought that you and Margaret were bonking each other's brains out all night, so why would I be roaming the streets of Perth looking for you?'

Following a couple more hour's kip, we gathered up our grubby clothes and wandered around the corner to a laundromat that we had spotted the day before. We grabbed a toasted sandwich and cup of tea from a nearby café while our clothes were washed and dried.

'Gotta find new digs today,' said Pete. 'I don't know about you, but my money's running out fast.'

'Yes, it's been great fun with those two birds, but geez, they have very fucking expensive tastes,' I replied.

That afternoon, we found a most helpful accommodation agency who located a couple of vacancies at a boarding house in the nearby suburb of Mount Lawley.

'It's clean, serves up good healthy food, and you can move in tomorrow,' said the pleasant agency lady, taking one week's rent in advance. 'It's called Jonkers Boarding House'.

After a modestly priced counter meal at a considerably less salubrious pub than we had being dining in with the girls, Pete and I walked back to the cinema where we had seen 'Benjamin' a few days before.

'Let's go see this one,' I said, looking at the poster for 'Pharaoh'. Nominated for Best Foreign Film at the Academy Awards, the poster boasted.

'I don't mind a bit of sword and sandal,' I joked.

Three hours later, two dejected souls wandered back to their hotel.

'One hundred and eighty bloody minutes of our lives completely wasted,' said Pete.

I couldn't help but agree. The entire movie seemed to consist of thousands of pale, scrawny actors running around in a sandy desert, yabbering to each other in Polish. We retired to bed early, hopeful that the weekend would produce a bit more fun.

7

WORKIN' AND FLIRTIN'

We checked out of the Deward very early (hooray – no more curfews) and checked in at our new home in Mount Lawley in time for breakfast. Jonkers Boarding House was run by an older aged couple of Dutch origin. It housed about a dozen guys. We were ushered into a large room, with six single beds spread out across the floor. There were also half a dozen old fashioned wooden wardrobes, and we were allocated one each for our belongings.

Shortly after our arrival, we made our way into a large kitchen with a huge table in the middle of the room. Blokes materialised suddenly, introduced themselves politely to Pete and I, as we all sat down expectantly at the table. The breakfast food was plain, but nutritious, and there was plenty of it.

'Eat as much as you like,' the bloke next to me said quietly. 'But don't take any food away from the table. Ma Jonkers has a fit if you take food to your room'.

After breakfast, a couple of us football nuts glued ourselves to the radio to listen to the VFL Grand Final being played on the famous MCG back in Melbourne. What a thriller it turned out to be. Over 116,000 spectators witnessed what sounded like one of the truly great Grand Finals played between Carlton and Essendon. The final winning margin of three points in favour of the Blues really had us on the edge of our seats.

'So, the Barassi magic has worked again,' said one of the other guys.

'Yep,' I replied. 'He's given the Blues their first flag in over in over 20 years. He really is proving to be a great coach'.

After an agreeable lunch, Pete and I grabbed a cab out to Subiaco to watch the local WAFL Grand Final. We were both pretty fired up after listening to the Victorian Grand Final, and keen to see some footy firsthand. The West Australian final was a very high standard game between the Perth Demons and the East Perth Royals. I watched the game intently, grabbing a local lad, and asking, 'Who's the muscular little rover playing for Perth?'

'That's Barry Cable,' he told me. 'Best bloody rover in Australia,' he added enthusiastically.

Indeed, Cable played a pivotal role in the game, which Perth eventually won comfortably by 24 points. The impressive Cable was adjudged best on ground, winning the Simpson Medal. 'I wonder how he'd go in the Victorian Football League?' I wondered out loud.

We returned to our new Mount Lawley abode in time to enjoy a good evening meal. Despite our two new female friends' unavailability, Pete and I were determined to enjoy our first Saturday night out in Perth. One of the guys in the boarding house suggested we try a night club called 'Wot the Hec', so we caught a cab to the venue. There was a lengthy queue outside, which Pete and I joined. It moved slowly, taking us a good twenty minutes before we eventually made it the front door, where we were met by two burly security guards. They looked down their combined noses imperiously.

'No tie, no entry,' they shouted at us, as if we were twenty feet away.

'You need to put up a sign mate,' said Pete. 'We've just wasted thirty minutes of our Saturday night for nothing.'

'Piss off,' came the curt reply.

'Wot the Hec' was immediately off our list of potential favourite venues.

We made our way to a different nightclub by the name of Firecracker. It too had had been recommended.

This was more like it. No problem getting in, and the crowd was grooving on the dance floor to a great sounding band. Impressed, I looked intently at the name of the band printed on the bass drum. 'The Beat N Tracks', I read out loud.

'Yeah,' yelled a bird close by. 'Best band in Perth by far', she added. Judging by what I was hearing, she couldn't be far wrong. We eventually made it back to Mount Lawley at around 1am and called it a night.

PETE and I rolled out of bed at 7am in time for breakfast, and then promptly returned to bed for a sleep in. After lunch we waited impatiently for Helen and Margaret to arrive, watching a boring old movie version of 'War and Peace' in the TV room to kill time.

The girls eventually arrived at around two o' clock in Margaret's car (yes, another Hillman Minx), both looking great.

'We thought we might drive up into the mountains,' suggested Margaret. 'We could head for the John Forrest National Park in the Darling Ranges.'

'Sounds good to me,' said Pete.

'We're completely in your hands,' I added flirtatiously.

As we drove, the conversation was light and cheerful, eventually leading to the inevitable question from the girls about our future travel plans.

'Well, we certainly want to make it a fair way up North, but we'll need to get jobs here in Perth to raise some more cash, before heading off,' I said.

'Oooh I'd love to go up North with you,' cooed Helen. 'Wouldn't that be exciting', she added, grinning suggestively to me.

After about a minute's silence, Helen hesitantly asked, 'And what type of jobs will you be applying for in Perth?'

'Oh, probably some labouring work,' replied Pete. 'If a bloke works a bit of overtime, he can still earn pretty good dough'.

'Really, labouring?' said Margaret with a slight twitch of her upper lip.

'How far to this park?' I asked, changing the subject.

It was obviously dawning on Margaret, that she really was flirting with rough trade, and wondering if this would continue to be exciting, or eventually become merely distasteful. The critical question for me was whether Helen still wanted to play dirty with someone from the wrong side of the tracks.

After driving for about forty minutes, we arrived at an elevated bush park. The awkwardness from the conversation a few moments before evaporated as we took in the splendid views across the countryside.

Margaret began rummaging in the boot of the car, passed out several LP records to Helen, and shoved a rectangular box under her arm, covering it with a raincoat. We made our way along some rather muddy tracks, eventually pausing in a beautiful clearing, resplendent with an even better vista than the one from the car park.

After parking our bums on the girl's raincoats, Margaret unpacked the rectangular box. Blow me if it wasn't a bloody record player.

'It's battery operated,' boasted Margaret, taking a Tom Jones long playing record out of its sleeve.

'I didn't know that anything like this existed,' I said in wonder as Tom Jones interrupted me with his booming Welsh voice to sing about how he would never fall in love again.

'I reckon that's his best song by far,' I ventured as Tom finished.

'Yes, it's good, but I still think I prefer Green Green Grass of Home,' opined Margaret.

'I think Bruce is really just being romantic,' intervened Helen, giggling.

That's my girl, I thought to myself, slipping my arm around Helen's waist.

The afternoon had a strange, yet warm atmosphere to it. Playing records, out in the open countryside and chatting amiably, proved to be a delight.

While Pete and Margaret continued to converse warmly enough, Helen and I cuddled and kissed with considerable passion all the way back to Mount Lawley in the back seat. I guess I had my answer about Helen wishing to play with a rough kid from the East. We made arrangements to meet again on the following Wednesday evening.

The next day at the Perth Labour Exchange proved fruitless. Returning to the boarding house I wrote long letters to Trish, the family, Gil, my brother Bob, and then posted them. Pete did likewise, inserting copies of his into the envelopes to Gil and Bob. That night I found watching TV unbearably boring. Was it the quality of the programs, or had I begun to prefer animated discussion, rather than sitting silently in front of an idiot box?

After an early breakfast, Pete and I headed straight back to the Labour Exchange.

'If we show up early again for a second straight day, they will know we're serious about wanting work,' said Pete confidently.

And so it proved to pass. Pete was immediately offered two days' work clearing up a work site. After an uncomfortable delay of 15 minutes or so, I was called back to the counter.

'This builder is looking for a labourer,' said the assistant, showing me a piece of paper with 'Sullivan and Sons' written on it. She then wrote down the address of a Girls High School. 'This is where they're working today,' she added. 'And you can easily catch a bus there from the stop over the road.

That was pretty easy, I thought happily.

I arrived at the nominated school's address after a 15 minute bus ride, and quickly strode through the gates making my way towards the cordoned off construction site. I walked up to a big bloke who appeared to be directing other blokes off in various directions with an assured authority. Before I had the opportunity to open my mouth, the big bloke turned on me. 'Are you the experienced labourer I asked for from the fuckin' labour exchange?' he bellowed at me.

'Well, yes,' I replied hesitantly.

'Okay, I need you mixing mud for the brickies pronto', he added, waving in the general direction of a machine that looked as though it may be used for mixing something in. I was about to ask what type of mud would be preferable, when the big bloke walked off bellowing further instructions to several other quivering underlings.

I approached the machine, observing that there was a big pile of sand on one side of it, and some very large paper bags piled up on the other side. I stood looking quizzically at the apparatus and materials. It must produce some type of building material. I guessed I was the person expected to make this minor miracle happen. Just then the big bloke bounded up, still full of life affirming self-importance.

'Well, what the fuck are you waiting for stupid?' he shouted at me.

'I think I might need a few instructions to get started,' I began apologetically.

'Jesus Christ,' said the big bloke to nobody in particular. 'Those bastards have sent me another bloody novice, and this one's got more hair than he knows what to do with'.

I was then ushered to a far corner of the construction site in shame. I was sure that if they had a large conical hat available, that I would be forced to wear it. One of the other burly big blokes sauntered over, and whilst he didn't wrap me up in his strong arms to console me, he did at least brusquely explain that the large pile of second-hand bricks needed cleaning. He picked one up with one hand, and with a hefty sized tomahawk, began to chip off the old mortar encrusted on each side of the brick.

'Got it?' he asked.

When I nodded, he added. 'Pile them neatly in stacks like the one over there, as you clean them.'

I set to work immediately, comforted with the knowledge that I was now a vital cog in the wheel of this mighty enterprise.

By morning tea, there wasn't a shred of skin left on the fingertips of my left hand. As I held painfully on to my mug of tea, an old guy sidled up to me. 'Here, use this to hold the brick,' he said giving me a square of thick rubber. 'Gloves wear out too quickly,' he added. 'So, when you start in a job like this you have to use something to protect your hands until they toughen up a bit.'

'Thanks', I said gratefully. I was indeed truly genuinely grateful that there appeared to be at least one other human being on this building site.

I returned to my corner and resumed my manly task. At the stroke of noon, the school bell rang. I had been told that our lunch break wasn't until 12.30, so I continued with my solitary task. I became aware of a group of pupils gathering on the edge of the roped off construction site. Glancing over, I could see a number of females roughly about my age, and that they were all focusing their attention squarely on me.

'Nice looking arse,' one blond haired bird said loudly.

'I'm more interested in the bulge in the front of his daks,' quipped the brunette next to her.

The other dozen or so girls laughed raucously.

'Never had an audience like this on the Nullarbor,' I thought, grinning to myself and leaning further into my job, greatly increasing the exposure of my bum crack. The crescendo of laughter was reaching even greater heights when the big bloke suddenly reappeared.

'No fucking around with the punters,' he growled at me.

'They started it,' I began to say, but was cut off abruptly when he repeated the warning.

Not long after I got back to the boarding house, Pete wandered down the road to the phone box to ring up Margaret. 'Helens got the flu,' he said to me when he returned. 'I hope it doesn't stuff up our date for Wednesday night'.

'I doubt I'd have the energy for a date anyway', I responded. I was in bed not long after dinner that night, sleeping like an infant, and dreaming of leering teenage girls, who were being enthusiastically cheered on by burly, red-faced workmen.

Over breakfast, Pete told me his first day of work was similar to my own. The only difference was that he was chipping off odd bits of extraneous concrete from a recently laid concrete floor.

'The most interesting part of my day was when about a dozen or so birds from the school decided to take an interest in me,' I told Pete. 'It was a bit of fun, but I'm not sure why they hung around for their entire lunchtime though.'

'Get off the grass, mate,' laughed Pete. 'How often do girls at school get to perve on a fit 18-year-old long haired blond guy, who was no doubt stripped to the waist, and sporting a deep tan?'

'S'pose so,' I said. 'I'd always assumed that perving on the opposite sex, was a guy's game. But now that I think about it, yesterday proved that girls like it too.'

As soon as I arrived at the work site I was again sent straight to my dismal corner, with nothing but a tomahawk and bricks for company. At least it gave me time to think. I had always believed that a labouring job required virtually no skills, but the day before had changed my opinion. I decided to spend some time watching the other guys working. The labourer with the mixing machine was making mortar for the brickies. I counted that the correct ratio of four shovels of sand to one of cement was about right. This was followed by the careful addition of water to get the right consistency. Another guy was taking the mortar from the mixer to the brickies in a wheelbarrow. I noticed he was pretty much running the whole time, in order to keep up with the demands of the tradies. The other guys running were two other labourers constantly filling their barrows with bricks. and hurrying to stack them up beside each brick layer.

Tough work, but at least I'll know what to do next time, I thought to myself.

At noon the school bell rang as usual, and the same group of birds came to stand and watch me intently, but this time they managed to get closer.

'Where ya from?' the same brunette who addressed me the day before, asked. 'Melbourne,' I responded with a smile.

'Oooh, he's from the big smoke,' said a blonde sheila.

My next moves were exercised with unrestrained egoism, combined with a marked lack of maturity.

'This really is hot work,' I exaggerated, taking off my shirt and grinning suggestively in the general direction of my female admirers. 'It sure is warmer in Perth than Melbourne.'

'Nice work if you can get it,' quipped one of the chicks, to which I winked and smiled while flexing my pecs by clenching the tomahawk.

So engaged was I with this flagrant flirtation, that I failed to notice that our activities were being intently watched by most of the guys on the work site. Suddenly a spontaneous round of cheering erupted from my work mates. I realised that the reaction from them was not one of admiration but was in fact intended to put me squarely back in my place. It was with a certain degree of humiliation that I turned my complete attention back to the ever so serious job of cleaning those bloody bricks. The girls giggled. For them the show wasn't over until they had to go back to class. I tried to ignore them.

As we were breaking up for the day, the big bloke turned to me and said, 'Do that again, and I'll kick your arse to Christmas, and back again.'

'Yes sir,' I replied, my face flushing red.

After dinner that night Pete went down the road to the phone box to ring Margaret. He came back quickly.

'Margaret's got the flu as well as Helen,' he said despondently. 'So, we won't be going out for a drink with them tonight.'

'That's okay with me,' I replied. 'I think I've had enough flirting with females for one day,' I added, as I settled down to watch the idiot box for the night.

Pete had been given the good news that his new employer was so happy with his work ethic, that he had been offered a permanent position.

'That's great news mate,' I enthused, secretly wishing that my own relationship with my employer was that good. I resolved not to allow myself to become so easily distracted.

Back at the work site, the big bloke strode out in front of a group of concreting specialists, and experienced labourers (plus one less experienced poor sod).

'The concrete trucks will arrive at regular intervals from 8 o 'clock, and you guys will barrow it to that long trench that was dug and prepared last week,' he explained, pointing to us labourers, and then to the said trench: 'You concreters know the drill from there. For those who don't already know,' he added looking directly at me. 'Time is bloody critical, so no fucking around. If we move too slowly, the concrete will set prematurely, and I'll get seriously angry'.

The first concrete truck arrived punctually at 8 and backed up to where we labourers stood with our wheelbarrows at the ready. Down the truck's open tube tumbled the pre-prepared moist concrete, into and filling the first bloke's wheelbarrow. Off he shot, running across the carefully laid out wooden planks towards the trench, and waiting concreters. My second workmate swung immediately into action, taking off with equal speed and energy as the first bloke as soon as his barrow was full. Then it was my turn. I maneuvered my own barrow into place, and once it was filled, I took off at speed. Christ it was heavy, and it took some real effort to keep it balanced as I ran full tilt to the trench. Having emptied it, it was straight back to get another load.

As the first truck ran out of concrete, a second one arrived, backed into place, and immediately began to fill our barrows, over and over again. By the time the third truck arrived my arm and leg muscles quivered and ached. The fitness levels I had acquired from my time on the Nullarbor were not up to the standard required here.

To add salt into my wounds, the big bloke yelled, 'No smoko this morning. I'll give you blokes an extra five minutes during the lunch break instead.'

I ploughed on, eventually tottering considerably, and noticeably slowing down. 'Move yourself Lowery,' bellowed the big bloke, without the slightest hint of sympathy.

Lunchtime eventually arrived and I sat shaking slightly,

sipping on my mug of tea and munching on one of Ma Jonker's door stopper sandwiches. I paid no attention to the group of devoted schoolgirls, who once again gathered on the sidelines. They were surely less impressed by the sadly broken youth on display today. I resumed my brick cleaning in the afternoon and kept myself to myself.

After my evening meal, it was my turn to wander down to the phone box. Helen came to the phone. She was obviously pleased to hear from me, but was still feeling rather poorly. She asked if I have any flu-like symptoms and was relieved to hear that I did not. It was obvious that we weren't going to be seeing each other for a while longer. I returned to Bonkers Brawling House and retired to bed early. I was absolutely knackered.

We rose early to enjoy one of the ever-reliable Ma Jonker's big breakfasts. Pete was in high spirits knowing that his job was to continue, and that the weekend beckoned. I felt a little less certain about things.

The big bloke greeted me on arrival at the work site with the joyful news that I was to be ferrying bricks to the brick layers for the day, with a couple of other labourers. We got started. The brickies got paid a piece rate and wouldn't tolerate a lack of bricks beside them. I started picking up two bricks at a time and placing them into my barrow. The bloke beside me noticed this.

'That's no good mate,' he said. 'It's best to pick up five or six in one go like this.'

My work companion then selected six bricks from the stack and picked them up by applying pressure to each of the end bricks, and then placing them neatly into the wheelbarrow. He continued until his barrow was full in a surprisingly quick time.

'You take them out of the barrow the same way the other end, which makes it easier to stack them for the brickie,' he said, taking off at speed, and making his way to an impatient looking brick layer.

I got into things, and soon started to find a rhythm. I couldn't quite keep up with the speed of the other two labourers, but I was at least improving. I concentrated on my job that day and was largely successful in managing to ignore some more smart comments from the ever-present group of female admirers.

At the day's end, the big bloke began passing out the pay packets to each of the work crew. After he had passed out all of the envelopes, bar one, he asked me to step away from the bunch of guys.

'We won't be needing you anymore after today,' he said passing me my pay packet. 'Firstly, you weren't experienced enough, but I could see you making an effort to learn late in the week,' he began. 'Likewise, you lacked condition, but that too was improving. But what I couldn't tolerate was the flirting with the schoolgirls. The last thing I need is a school kid up the duff from one of my workers,' the big bloke stated with a heavy emphasis on the 'up the duff' bit. 'So, my parting advice is, SEX and THE WORKPLACE DON'T MIX,' the boss concluded, loudly enough for most of the other workers to hear clearly.

As he walked away, he casually added over his shoulder, 'By the way, I've popped an extra two bob in your pay packet for you to go and get a haircut, so don't waste it'.

After a relaxed Saturday morning breakfast Pete went into town to buy some socks, while I sulked around, feeling sorry for myself. Arriving back for lunch, Pete tried to cheer me up.

'You've got to put these things down to experience,' he said philosophically. 'Anyway, by the sounds of things, you stuffed it up for yourself, by thinking with your dick again,' he added. 'Let's go to the pub for a few beers this afternoon,' he continued quickly. 'You'll feel better in no time'.

Now that was advice I understood perfectly.

Pete and I walked to the Rosemount Hotel in North Perth and settled in at the bar for a few quiet beers. We chatted about our work experiences from the past week for a while, but then began to join in with many other discussions with numerous locals, gaining further valuable inside information about Perth.

Eventually we made our way back to Jonkers, wobbling a bit along the footpath. Suddenly I noticed some beautiful roses growing in the front yard of a splendid looking residence. Parts of the rose bushes overhung the fence line with the flowers growing at a tempting height. Emboldened by the influence of alcohol, I deduced that if the flowers were outside the property's border, they would be free to any passer-by, so I picked a small bunch of the most perfectly formed red flowers. Ma Jonkers was most surprised by my clumsy attempt at chivalry.

AFTER DINNER, Pete sensibly announced that he had had enough booze for one day, and that he was going to the flicks to see Doctor Zhivago.

'It was released a couple of years ago,' he said. 'And this could be the last opportunity I have to see it on the big screen'.

I rather less sensibly stated that I was up for a bloody good night out on the town.

Les and John were two likely lads from the boarding house, who were also looking for a lively Saturday night. After a few more beers at the North Perth pub, we all grabbed a cab, and headed for Pinocchio's. There was a duo playing by the name of 'Pieces of Eight' who specialised in songs by the Everly Brothers, Simon and Garfunkel and other similar musos. They were well into an excellent version of 'Cathy's Clown' when we arrived and sat down. By the time they had started singing 'Walk Right Back', Les, John and I had left our beers on our table and were dancing with some crazy chicks. As the girls joined us for a drink, I asked the bird I'd been dancing with if she knew anything about the band. 'They get quite a few gigs around town and are very popular,' she replied.

'Flashy dressers too,' I added, looking at their unusual brightly coloured shirts, each with a large buckle (of all things) at the neck. 'Whatever,' I said. 'They have great harmonies and cover some really good songs very well.'

The atmosphere in the nightclub was terrific. Good music, good dancing and even better beer. As closing time approached in the early hours of the morning, I yelled over to my boarding house cobbers, 'I'm bloody starving. Where can we get something to eat?'

'Bernies,' came the unanimous reply from punters.

We all bundled into some bird's car and drove down the road in the direction of Kings Park. I realised that I was getting to know my way round, even in this considerably inebriated state. We parked in front of Bernies, ordered a hamburger and fries each, and continued drinking beer.

'This place is a legend,' rejoiced one of my less than sober companions.

He was right. The burgers were sensational.

Somehow, someone who was at least relatively sober, offered to drive Les, John and I back to Mount Lawley.

'Serially good uv yoo,' John slurred at our patient benefactor.

It was close to 3am when the three of us burst into 'Bonkers', turning on all the lights in the bedroom, and wishing everyone our most sincere best wishes (or something like that). A previously sleeping boarder called out, 'Turn the fucking lights off.'

We did so, falling, giggling and farting our way to our beds.

THE DAY BEGAN with Pete shaking me awake.

'It's breakfast time ya silly bugger,' he announced, with a tad too much jollity and volume.

'No need to shout,' I responded, holding my head in my hands. 'You go on. I'll be right behind you,' I croaked, immediately falling back to sleep.

I eventually awoke at close to lunchtime with a bladder that was set to explode and a thirst that would have given Burke and Wills a run for their money. After attending to these two high priorities, I showered and made my way gingerly to the dining table. I looked over to see Les. His face was an awful lot paler than I remembered but looked almost tanned in comparison to John's when he also eventually staggered into the dining room. In an attempt to appear that I was recovering, I turned to Pete. 'How was Doctor Jukargo….er Zavacko mate?'

'Christ,' he responded. 'You're still bloody pissed'.

By about 2pm, I had sobered up enough to agree with Pete's clever suggestion that we walk our legs off to see the sights of the fine city of Perth. We took off at pace, walking through Northbridge and the CBD, finally arriving at the magnificent Langley Park.

It was a beautiful sunny day, which brought out the best of a wonderful open space beside the Swan River. It had taken us just over an hour, and I was by now, completely sober. After enjoying the many sights of Langley Park, we walked back by a slightly different route, running slap bang into the delightful Hyde Park, with its shady trees and grassed area. We arrived back in Mount Lawley tired, but both agreeing that it had been really worthwhile getting to know that lovely city a good deal better.

After we returned, a group of inmates gathered in the back garden, enjoying a smoke, while we waited for dinner to be announced. Suddenly one of the tenants rushed into the garden with his transistor in hand.

'It's the new Beatles song,' he yelled excitedly. Without exception we all gathered around listening intently. The slow build-up of 'Hey Jude' had us totally captivated, and by the time the song reached 'Na Na Nana Na' chorus we were mesmerized. After the music finished, I looked over at Pete. 'You may think I'm a bit premature mate, but I think that is their best effort yet.'

'I bloody well think you're spot on,' he replied.

'And what happened to the job we found you last week?' asked the prim faced employment advisor, as I stood before him.

'Well, I think they had somebody return back from being ill,' I lied. 'I'm up for anything you've got now though.'

'Go and sit down,' said my clearly indifferent, employment specialist friend.

I obeyed. I sat, and sat, and sat. By mid-morning I approached the desk again.

'Nope, nothing today,' came the abrupt reply from the same specialist irritably.

I bit my tongue, said nothing, and walked back to the boarding house to watch television with the house cat.

After returning the next morning to the Labour Exchange the same poker faced employee greeted me with the same dead pan expression but at least the news was more favourable. 'I've got two or three days work in a factory, covering for someone who's off sick,'. 'Are you able to go straight there?'

The bus took me to within a couple of streets of the factory I'd been sent to. It was a sizeable place and they appeared to be manufacturing large steel prefabricated building objects of varying sizes.

I was directed to the site office, where the foreman looked me up and down quizzically. 'You seem to be in pretty good shape young fella,' he said in a friendly enough tone. 'Our Joe is a bit crook with a tummy bug or something, so we'll need you to fill in for him, until he comes back,' he continued. 'Come out the back, and I'll show you all about the job'.

As we walked towards the rear of the factory, my affable new boss chatted to me about the various large steel objects being welded together expertly by my soon-to-be workmates. I could only hear about every second or third word, because of the noise in the place, so was really none the wiser about what was actually going on.

Eventually, we emerged from the back of the factory into a small enclosed outside area. On a sidewall there was a large stack of thick solid steel RSJ beams, each a good five metres long.

'Joe cuts these buggers into specific lengths for us, so that'll be your job,' said the foreman, grabbing one of the RSJs, and lifting it onto a couple of strategically placed stands.

At one end of one of the stands I could see, of all things, a saw. The foreman measured off specific lengths of the beam with a tape measure, marking them precisely with a ruler and a thick builder's pencil. He then manoeuvred the beam along, aligning the marked cutting line with the saw blade, and locking it into place with some vices. He then pushed a button that started a small pump. Out ran a stream of white oil, splashing over the cutting area of the RSJ beam, and falling into a receptacle immediately underneath, where it was recycled back in a continuous flow. He then started the saw, lowering the blade onto the RSJ. We then stood back watching as the saw slowly cut its way through the steel beam. It took a good twenty minutes to finally cut its way through. We then reset the RSJ for another cut.

'You have to keep watching all the way through the cutting process in case there is a jam,' the foreman informed me. 'You can't go off for a piss or anything else, once the cutting process starts.'

I nodded. Setting up for each cut took no more than three minutes. There then followed a good twenty minutes of me twiddling my thumbs while watching the monotonous cutting process, and then repeating the exercise, over, and over again.

Surely this must be in the Guinness Book of Records under the section, 'Most Boring Jobs in the World', I thought to myself.

During the lunch break, I sat down next a few of my new work buddies with a brew of tea in one hand, and a large Jonkers-style sandwich in the other.

'I'm filling in for Joe while he's off crook,' I said, introducing myself.

'Yeah, I hope he recovers soon,' replied the welder beside me. 'I reckon he's worked here for more than twenty years.'

'Not doing the same job?' I asked half-jokingly.

'Yep, always the same, never done anything else, as far as I know,' the welder replied.

I choked on a bit of my sandwich. How could he have stood the monotony for all those years?

I arrived back at the boarding house to find letters from my Mum and Dad which gave a sharp reminder that things were tough at home, but despite this I was still in their thoughts. Mum wrote:

The children are in bed early tonight. Poor old Dad took them to the Dental Hospital yesterday, as all four of them needed work done. He thought that it would be cheaper. Well, it wasn't. They charged $3 for each tooth, and they were kept waiting for ages!

We all think of you both often and wish you all the luck in the world. Glad you like your new digs.

I READ over Dad's letter to me.

> *You went without your Sheaffer pen (the green one). I've had it fixed up and have used it successfully in business lately. Can I borrow it permanently? Feel it brings me luck and is a fond reminder of you.*
>
> *You're always in my heart son. I love you very much you know. Take care always till you're safely home again to us.*

Pete and I returned to the boarding house after both of us had completed very tedious work duties throughout the next day. Pete had been digging trenches, which proved very frustrating.

'The bloody soil is so sandy,' he complained, 'that the walls keep falling in.'

'Better than sawing through fucking RSJ's' all day,' I replied, pipping him by a considerable margin, in my humble opinion.

After the evening meal, I walked down to the phone box and rang Helen. 'Great news Pete,' I said enthusiastically upon returning to the boarding house. 'Both Helen and Margaret have fully recovered from the flu and would like to take us the Drive In tomorrow night.'

'What a bloody bottler,' Pete said happily.

'They said they'll pick us up at 7.30.'

Another romantic session with the gorgeous Helen would more than make up for the shitty work conditions I'd been suffering through.

It was only after chasing up our dates with the two girls that I checked the mail table and found that we had another letter arrive. It was from my big brother Bob. He'd addressed it to the both of us, as he was friendly with Pete too.

> I've finished my initial National Service training at Puckapunyal, and have now started four weeks of Corps training, which consists mostly of driving the Mark III's and Land Rovers. After that I start on the Air Dispatch course. We will be working with Caribous and various types of helicopters, learning about dropping supplies by parachute. After that I'll be off doing a parachuting course myself. We'll do about eight jumps in three weeks, which I'm rather looking forward to.
>
> I think I'll be going to Vietnam in March but will be pretty busy before then.
>
> By the way Bruce, I saw Trish at the pictures whilst on leave last weekend (she was with another girl). She said to tell you that her parents were blocking your letters to her, so could you send them to someone else here, who can pass them on to her.

'Seems that Bob's doing well in the Army, judging by his letter,' said Pete. 'All that training sounds really tough but interesting, and he'll get a lot of extra pay when he goes to Nam.'

'Yeah, I'm genuinely pleased for him,' I responded. 'It seems that there are some rewards from the Army for Nasho's, if you're prepared to work hard'.

'It's a dirty trick by Trish's parents by withholding your letters though mate,' said Pete compassionately.

'I'll get around it,' I said.

I was angry and upset. To be honest, I didn't know how I would get around it. Trish would think that she was fading from my thoughts.

As I was about to leave the factory at 4 o'clock the next day, the foreman called me over.

'I've just heard from Joe that he's recovered okay, and will be back at work on Monday,' he said, passing me a pay envelope. 'I wanted to thank you for the past three days, but I'm afraid I have no further work for you.' I said that I understood and walked towards the bus stop. It was good news for Joe, and even better news for me. If I had one more day working there, I may have put my own neck under that frigging saw blade.

Helen and Margaret arrived punctually at 7.30pm, and in separate cars again.

'Great,' I whispered to Pete, as we walked towards the girl's cars. 'That means we'll have a bit more personal space for some serious snogging.'

'Jump in guys,' yelled Margaret. 'We're going to see 'The Thomas Crown Affair' with Steve McQueen, so there's sure to be a long queue.' I jumped in beside Helen, giving her a lingering kiss on the neck. 'Enough of that you two,' bawled Margaret. She then pulled out onto the road as soon as Pete's bum had hit the seat. We followed on.

The queue hadn't been so bad. We'd stopped for a couple of cans of vodka and lemon for the girls, as well as a couple of cans of Emu Bitter for us, and still managed to park the cars side by side at the drive-in.

The movie plot had millionaire sportsman Steve McQueen

masterminding a huge bank robbery. Of course, he doesn't need the dough, because he already has money coming out of his ears. He just does it for fun. Enter the fabulous Faye Dunaway as the clever and sexy insurance investigator Vicki. The plot has both Helen and I really intrigued, so we watched it intently while sitting close.

Suddenly the sex scenes were becoming pretty full on and I gradually became aware that Helen's hand was nestling on my thigh. That's it! Bugger the movie. Steve bloody McQueen can look after things for himself. We kissed passionately, enthusiastically employing the two-tongue-tango method.

Christ, this girl really was randy.

Her hand was now firmly on my crotch, and my hands were caressing parts of her anatomy that had previously been strictly off limits.

Boy oh boy, it was getting very hot in the kitchen (or in this case, in the Hillman's cabin).

Suddenly, the back door of the car opened, and someone firmly sat down on the back seat.

'Bloody woman,' said a familiar voice. I reluctantly took a break from what I had been doing, and looked over Helen's shoulder to see Pete, sitting bolt upright with his arms folded. 'What's happened mate?' I said, trying not to sound frustrated.

'Well Margaret kept telling me what she thought was going to happen next in the movie, so I told her to shut up.'

'Oh no,' whispered Helen. 'Margaret won't stand for that'.

I glanced over at the other car through our steamed-up passenger side window and could have sworn I saw Margaret mouthing something vaguely obscene towards Helen's back seat, her face contorted with extreme rage. She then returned the speaker to its stand, and drove her car somewhat erratically towards the exit, while vigorously winding up her car window.

Helen, Pete and I then tried to focus on the end of the movie, but I found it difficult to concentrate. The drive back to Mount Lawley took place in silence. As Helen stopped the car outside our boarding house, Pete thanked her, and quickly jumped out, striding towards the front door. I moved closer to Helen, kissing her sweetly.

'Sorry Bruce,' she said sadly, 'but the moment has passed.'

'I suppose so,' I said with a heavy heart and fading erection. 'Maybe next time we'll get lucky.'

I left the car and waved forlornly to the object of my affection as I walked away. We both felt a certain despair over our still unconsummated love affair.

The next morning, I still felt more than a little angry. I had 'kept my powder dry', from the previous night. When I had followed Pete inside, all the other guys were asleep, so I thought it best to discuss things in the morning. Pete suggested we pop outside into the garden just before breakfast. Once outside, I took a deep breath, and was about to unleash my bottled-up tirade about him letting a mate down, when Pete got in first.

'Shit Bruce, I'm so sorry about last night,' said my mate with such a genuine look of sorrow on his dial, that it completely took the wind out of my sails. 'I admit that I was probably a bit abrupt with Margaret last night, but I didn't see bloody World War Three coming,' he went on. 'Christ that woman has a temper and a mouth like Genghis Khan on a bad day. When she said get out of the car, I had no choice, and where else could I go, but into the car with you and Helen?'

I could see there was no point being angry, but I couldn't resist one last dig. 'Okay let's forget about it,' I said, 'but next time that happens, you had better choose to walk home.

After breakfast, a few of the blokes went out into the garden for a smoke. I spotted a young guy sitting on his own on a garden seat, so I went over for a chat.

'Ken, isn't it?' I asked. 'Yes Bruce, that's me', said the young bloke in a high voice. I figured he couldn't be much older than 16.

'How come a young bloke like you lives here in a boarding house, and not at home with your Mum and Dad?' I asked showing great concern for the young loner.

'Piss off,' came the immediate and rude reply. 'How old do you think I am?' said Ken fiercely.

'About sixteen.'

'I'm bloody well twenty-six,' Ken almost shouted.

'Pull the other leg mate,' I laughed.

With that Ken leapt from his chair and walked quickly back into the house.

I walked over to where Pete was chatting with a few other fellas.

'I appear to have upset that young bloke Ken,' I said.

But before Pete could answer, Ken reappeared, waving a thick leather object in my direction. He stood in front of me and opened his wallet. He pulled out a copy of his driver's license, and thrust it into my hand, without saying a word. I read it quickly.

'Shit Ken, you're actually nearly twenty-seven,' I said incredulously.

There was a hush in the conversation from the other guys too, as they listened in. Ken produced another document. This time it was a copy of his birth certificate, which again proved that our Kenny's balls had probably dropped more than a dozen years before.

'Okay Ken, I'm sorry. I obviously made a mistake.'

But bloody Kenny wasn't finished. He produced another prized document with even greater dramatic flourish. This document was a copy of a frigging tax return, which, yet again, proved that Ken's time on this earth exceeded a quarter of a century.

Ken was fishing in his wallet for yet another document when I said, 'Okay Ken you've made your point,' as I backed away towards the house.

As I was about to turn away, my protagonist whipped out a fourth piece of paper from his wallet and began to shake it in my face. I fled indoors.

That night, Pete and I went to Pinocchio's after popping into the Melbourne Hotel for a few beers. We were both beginning to like the night club quite a bit. There was always a half decent band playing, and you could always get a dance with the many chicks who seemed to flock there. I looked over at the band. They were a four-piece unit called The Revue. Their version of the Box Tops 'The Letter' was pretty darn good.

I was tapping my toes and checking out the birds on the dance floor, when I suddenly noticed a security guy near the front door talking earnestly to Ken from the boarding house. He was shaking his head. I continued watching as I saw Ken begin to take out the first document from his wallet. For the first and only time, I felt sympathy for a night club security guard.

8

ENTER BIG BOB

When Bob Manders arrived at Jonkers Boarding House one morning, he was told to bunk in the same room as Pete and I. He was a big friendly bloke with a black sense of humour. As soon as I jokingly introduced Pete and I as two young adventurers emanating from the civilized world of Melbourne, I discovered that he was disarmingly direct and laugh-out-loud funny.

'Stone the flamin' crows,' Bob said in a booming voice. 'Two wise men from the East, eh?'

Bob had been about a good bit, and while he joked about things almost continually, he was obviously nobody's fool. Conversation with him was often laced with a fair sprinkling of 'fair dinkum's, 'bloody oath's and 'she'll be apples', or similar Australian vernacular. I warmed to him immediately.

The three of us took off that afternoon for a long walk into Perth CBD, yacking and laughing the whole way. We decided to go and see the great Johnny O'Keefe at the Cats Whisker nightclub that night, where it would be possible to have a few beers on an otherwise dry Sunday.

The three of us entered the front doors of the Cats Whisker, but only after a lengthy interrogation by two abrasive security guards.

It was Bob who broke the ice with them saying, 'Fair go guys, I'm so hungry I could eat the arse out of a low flying duck.'

The tension evaporated immediately, and we paid the exorbitant entrance fee. We found a table in the darkened atmosphere and bypassed the hugely expensive dinner menu to head straight for the bar.

'My shout,' said Pete, ordering three cans of Swan Lager.

As we sat back down at our table Pete looked at the change the bartender had given him.

'Fuck,' he cried. 'I've just paid fifty cents for each can of beer.'

'Fifty bloody cents,' I repeated, gobsmacked.

But once we had finished our first cold foaming beverage, we managed to overcome our shock sufficiently to keep ordering more. The Cats Whisker was one of the few places where you could get a drink on a Sunday night, and they probably had to pay J O K a lot to perform, we reasoned.

As we sat supping on our 'gold standard' beers and discussing O'Keefe's career, the dim lighting started to get darker still. For eighteen-year-olds like us, J O K was a performer from a bygone era. He hadn't had a top ten hit for almost half a decade. Nevertheless, we still spoke reverently about him. He was Australia's first real rock and roller from the 50's and early 60's.

It was pitch black when a voice boomed through the speakers.

'Ladies and Gentlemen, put your hands together for the great, and one and only, Johnny O'Keefe.'

A spotlight lit up the unmistakable image of the wild one, all decked out in a black tuxedo. His hands were behind his back as he stepped up to the microphone, tilted his head back slightly, and backed by an excellent four-piece band, began to sing.

The voice was raspy, but loud. Occasionally he missed reaching the odd high note too, but his commanding presence was extraordinary.

The audience was ecstatic, and my spine began to tingle. The end of the song was met with deafening applause, as he immediately launched straight into 'Shake Baby Shake', followed by 'So Tough'. His old hits kept coming, one after another. By the time he was belting out 'Shout', the crowd was on its feet, jumping up and down and clapping in time with the beat.

His ballads too were greeted just as warmly, as he crooned raggedly through 'I'm Counting on You' and 'She Wears my Ring'. What a performer! There was no doubting that he held the crowd right in the palm of his hand that night. The performance was nothing short of electrifying.

It was well past midnight as we walked unsteadily outside, filled with grossly overpriced beer and blinking like deers at the passing car headlights. We eventually hailed a cab and tumbled in, raucously singing J O K hits at the top of our voices. The taxi driver grinned amiably enough as he sped his cab towards Mount Lawley. I guess he felt we were harmless enough, and at least we were happy.

'Bloody glad we don' ave to get up hearly Bob,' I slurred.

'Pish off,' yelled Pete. 'I gotta get up at six.'

'Don't wake us up,' Bob and I chorused.

It was well past 1am when we stumbled into our bedroom, making very loud shooshing noises towards each other, with our index fingers to our lips. Silly bloody idiots!

. . .

I BECAME aware of the bed shaking vigorously when I finally opened my eyes late the next morning. I felt bloody crook.

'Stop shaking the fucking bed,' I moaned.

Silence. The shaking continued.

I opened one eye to see that the wall of the bedroom was shaking alarmingly. A picture on the wall fell off with a crash.

'Get out of the house!' someone yelled.

I tumbled out of bed and sprinted out into the garden, naked except for my jocks, which struggled to adequately contain my nocturnally half aroused penis.

Ma and Pa Jonkers, Bob plus three or four unemployed tenants stood watching the swaying house, with their mouths collectively wide open. Eventually Bob became aware of my presence.

'Great exit boyo,' he beamed, looking me up and down, with his eyes finally resting on my nether region. 'Nice to see you rise to the occasion too.'

I could do little but stand there with my hands on my hips, acutely aware of the tut-tutting sounds emanating from Ma Jonkers.

Once the earthquake appeared to have subsided, I raced inside to pull on a pair of daks. The rest of the crowd cautiously re-entered the house and turned on the telly to find out that a 6.5 magnitude earthquake had been centred on the small country town of Meckering.

'Bit of a shaky start to the day,' commented Bob drily.

Although it was 120 kilometres away, the force of it in Mount Lawley had been powerful. Indeed, the media was reporting considerable damage to many buildings in the Perth CBD. Meckering itself was absolutely flattened.

We remained in a state of shock for some hours.

I spent the afternoon writing a letter to Trish that I would send to my mate Gil for delivery. I wrote to my family and a couple of other mates too.

I then rang Helen to see if she and her family were affected by the quake. She confirmed that all was okay but seemed a little distant. I was getting the feeling that she wasn't interested in going on another date. I guessed that the continual frustrations were having a negative effect.

Pete arrived back from work looking absolutely knackered. He wandered off to his bed almost straight after dinner. I glared at the black and white images on the idiot box with Bob for a short while before also succumbing to the need for sleep.

I prised myself out of bed early the next day to join Pete for breakfast. I needed to get to the Labour Exchange at opening time to find a job. My money was starting to run out. Bob joined us at the breakfast table too. He was usually a late riser.

'Ripsnorter breakfast this morning,' he boomed as he wolfed down his fourth slice of toast and reached for a fifth.

'Leave some for the other punters mate,' I said, laughing. 'Ma Jonkers will need to do another bakery run.'

As Pete rushed out the door to meet his lift to work, Bob and I followed him out the door. 'Don't forget us dear,' said Bob in his saddest voice whilst wiping his eyes with a large red handkerchief.

'Never mind all that,' I added in a mock stern voice. 'No stopping at the pub on the way home.'

'Piss off you two,' yelled Pete over his shoulder, as he ran to a waiting car.

'You shouldn't be so harsh on our boy,' Bob said to me in his best attempt at a high-pitched housewife voice.

Bob and I arrived at the Labour Exchange a good 15 minutes before opening time, which was just as well. There was already about ten blokes there before us. Jobs were obviously getting tight around Perth. Eventually I was called up to the counter to be greeted by the same dweeb that I had seen the last time.

'You again,' said my employment mentor in a strangely flat voice that still managed to express maximum irritation. Had he ever smiled?

'Most employers don't like young men with such long hair,' he continued wiping his hand over his own greasy but short locks.

'Nothing today for you – NEXT,' he bellowed to the waiting crowd.

I walked outside with my tail between my legs. Bob followed me out. He'd seen another staff member.

'Any luck Bob?' I said hopefully.

'Nah, the bloke I saw had a few kangaroos loose in the top paddock,' he replied. 'You?'

'I saw Mister Charisma again,' I said pessimistically. 'He wouldn't give me the steam off his piss'.

'Let's grab a paper to see what jobs are advertised in there,' suggested Bob.

We sat on a park bench with *The West Australian* newspaper spread out in front of us. Unsurprisingly the headlines that day were – QUAKE HAVOC: 20 HURT. Below the headline there was a startling picture of what appeared to be the ruins of a pub in Meckering. Subheadings of SUPPLIES SENT, and GRIM STORIES revealed the utter devastation that had happened in that wheat belt town located 54 miles east of Perth. 'Poor bastards,' said Bob in a serious voice for once.

Turning the pages to the employment section, we began to scan through the jobs available. Near the top was a neat ad located in its own squared off area. It immediately aroused our interest.

JACKAROOS WANTED: LARGE SHEEP STATION LOCATED NEAR SHARK

BAY ON THE NORTH WEST COAST OF WA REQUIRES THE SERVICES OF SEVERAL FIT YOUNG MEN.
GOOD PAY, FULL BOARD AND TRANSPORT TO LOCATION PROVIDED.
CONTACT: SHEFFIELD EMPLOYMENT
SHEFFIELD HOUSE
713 HAY STREET, PERTH
TELEPHONE 23 3537

'That's for us mate,' yelled Bob, punching my arm in excitement. 'You ring through though; you've got a better telephone voice.'

We found a telephone box. I slotted in the necessary coins and dialled the number.

'Sheffield Employment, Jean Munro speaking,' said a mature sounding female voice.

I explained that I was ringing about the Jackaroo ad in today's paper, that there were two of us very interested, and that we would be available to start immediately.

'Very good,' replied Jean. 'Would you be able to come in to see us tomorrow at 10am?' Would we ever! I gave Jean both our names and the address of the boarding house, confirming that we would be in their office promptly at 10 the next day.

That night I tried to bring Pete around to the idea.

'It's a golden opportunity for us to travel north, which is where we want to head anyway,' I enthused. 'And someone will pay the fair and give us a job with full board when we get there,' I continued in a rush. 'What could go wrong?'.

Pete thought for a moment. 'Look, I'm getting good pay at the moment in a secure job,' he said carefully. I reckon I might take the opportunity to save a few dollars, and then join you blokes up north a little bit later.'

'Yep, I understand mate,' I replied. 'But it would be a shame to split up the old team.' Pete agreed that was true, but sensibly stuck to his guns.

Bob and I caught the bus into the CBD, and we found ourselves at 713 Hay Street by 9.50am. The business in front of us was named Caris Brothers, but we soon found a plaque for Sheffield Employment on the wall that led us to a small narrow stairway. We walked upstairs and into the waiting room of our prospective employment saviours. An immaculately dressed receptionist greeted us.

'Mr Lowery and Mr Manders, I presume?' she smiled. 'Please take a seat and fill out these medical declaration forms.'

I scanned through the list of questions, and without exception ticked the NO box to all declarations about ailments that I may have suffered from previously in my relatively short life. These included tuberculosis, heart condition, mental illness, back problems or any sexually transmitted diseases (listing gonorrhoea and syphilis as examples).

I was beginning to ponder the relativity of this last question regarding our suitability for a job tending to the needs of sheep, when my thoughts were interrupted by the voice of the receptionist.

'Miss Munro will see you now.'

We were ushered into a large old-fashioned office, complete with a large impressive looking wooden desk, and several leather encased chairs in front of it. Seated behind the desk in an even larger leather chair, was a neat looking middle-aged woman. The plaque on the desk declared that we were seeing the great Miss Munro herself.

'Mister Lowery and Mister Manders?' she asked, but without waiting for a reply continued. 'Thank you both for being here punctually at 10am. May I see your medical forms?'

After scanning through them, she paused, and looking over the top of her heavily framed glasses, asked 'You both appear remarkably fit and healthy young men? Not so much as a cold, it would appear?' Both Bob and I beamed back at her nodding like two demented friends of Big Ears. 'And you're ready to start immediately?'

'Yes,' both of us replied in unison.

'The pay is $28.10 gross, which equates to $19 after tax, but with full board included. The station owners advise that no experience is necessary, but the work is physically hard,' she went on. 'Your bus will leave at 6am from the main Perth Bus Terminal this coming Saturday. Is that acceptable to you both?'

'Does that mean that our applications have been accepted?' I stammered. 'Yes, yes,' said Miss Munro almost dismissively. 'Just sign these contracts', she added, thrusting two clearly pre-prepared documents in front of Bob and I.

The contract looked to be completely in line with our discussion, so I signed my copy before Miss Munro had time to change her ever so generous mind. Bob did likewise.

As we were leaving, I paused. 'The contract says that we will be employed at Yaringa Station?'

'Yes,' Miss Munro answered with a hint of irritation, her right eyebrow raised.

'Where exactly is it located?' I asked, ever so politely.

'Just south of Carnarvon, near Shark Bay,' she replied before returning to her work. Bob and I exchanged glances and shrugged. Where the fuck was that?

We left the fine offices of Sheffield Employment and made a beeline for a newsagent to buy a map of West Australia.

'Shit, that's all right,' I said excitedly to Bob. 'It's about 900 kilometres north of Perth, and right on the coast.'

'The further away the better,' replied Bob somewhat enigmatically.

After breakfast, I scribbled out a letter for Trish that would hopefully reach her via my trusty couriers, as well as letters to my folks and a few mates, telling them about my move north, and the address they should send any letters to. I completed them just in time to catch the early collection time from the post box down the street. After showering I stood looking at myself in the mirror. I loved my long hair, but sensibly realised that it could be many months before I would be anywhere near a hairdresser again. By that time my hair might be past my shoulders!

Time to bite the bullet, I thought.

I strode out to a nearby barbers before I had time to reconsider.

Barber Bill's was in a nearby shopping strip.

'Just a bit of a trim please mate,' I instructed the barber.

He was a man of slight stature, dressed in a considerably oversized white coat, who stood attentively by my chair, almost feverishly clutching a pair of scissors and a comb. It was as if I could read his mind: 'I've been waiting for years for the opportunity to give a proper haircut to a Nancy boy like this.'

Before I could protest, my blond locks were floating towards the floor. The brutal attack lasted no more than 10 minutes, with Bill finally stepping back to examine his handiwork, his face beaming with undiluted satisfaction. I stared at my image in the mirror on the wall in front of me.

'Shit! Who was that guy?' My hair had not been that bloody short for frigging years.

OVER BREAKFAST THE FOLLOWING DAY, Bob and I decided that we badly needed some new gear for the work up north. 'Solid boots,' said Bob simply enough.

'And a hat,' I added enthusiastically.

'There's an army disposal shop in Barrack Street,' Bob suggested. 'Let's go there after brekkie.'

After catching a bus into town, Bob and I were striding down

Barrack Street towards the army disposal shop, skylarking with each other like two slightly demented clowns, when we were stopped in our tracks by two guys in suits and wearing trilby hats. They stepped right in front of us.

'Hello Bob,' said one of the interlopers. 'Where are we off to then?'

'None of your business,' I said, taking a step towards them.

'Let it go Bruce,' said Bob, grabbing my arm.

Two more suited blokes also suddenly appeared from another direction. They marched me about 10 yards down the street, while Bob was being forced to face a shop wall with his hands touching it palms down, and his feet spread out wide, by the first two assailants. They were roughly frisking him.

'What's your name then buddy?' asked one of my allotted aggressors.

They appeared satisfied enough with my answers, but had written everything down carefully in a notebook, which annoyed me.

The original two suits seemed to be letting Bob remove himself from the wall, when I clearly heard one of them say loudly, 'Don't leave town Bob. We'll be wanting to talk with you again very soon.' Bob nodded quietly, and the four suits walked briskly away.

'Who the fuck...,' I started to say to Bob, feeling more than a little violated. 'Leave it Bruce,' repeated Bob emphatically.

'But who were those guys?' I insisted. 'Well, there's the police, and then there are the real police,' he explained. 'Those guys are the real ones, and you don't fuck with them,' Bob concluded.

'Well, we weren't doing anything wrong, so they shouldn't be hassling us,' I said naively.

'Look Bruce, there are some things you don't know about

me, and don't really need to know,' explained Bob. 'Suffice to say those coppers have it in for me.'

'Okay mate,' I replied. 'Enough said'. We walked on towards the army disposal store in silence. I felt more than a little unsettled.

Inside the shop we selected some elastic-sided leather work boots, and I decided to also buy an ex-diggers slouch hat for added protection against the sun. I counted the money left in my wallet. There was just enough to buy a knife. I selected a large black handled one with its own sheath. I hadn't the foggiest idea of why I thought I needed a weapon such as this. It just seemed like a good idea.

AFTER DINNER that night I rang Helen to let her know about my job up north and that I would be leaving in the morning. She wished me well and then politely ended the conversation by explaining that Margaret had just arrived, and that they were going out together for a few drinks. I was definitely getting the 'brush off', so there was to be no last minute nooky as a parting gift. The girl had no heart.

Pete and I wandered around to the nearest pub for a few quiet beers, and to reminisce about our travels thus far. We were a bit down to be parting company but reassured ourselves that we would soon team up again. We would make sure of it. After enjoying a few pots, we headed back to Ma Jonkers. It was going to be an early start the next day.

Bruce and his good mate Gil, aged 18.

My mum (Effie), Dad (Robert), my brother Bob and myself. This photo was taken shortly after emigrating to Australia from England (I'm the short arse kid).

My travelling buddy Pete outside the Derwood Hotel.

Showing off my hitch hiking techniques for the camera.

Yaringa Station from afar - circa 1968.

Yaringa.

Pete Lawrance (left), the author and Barry Brogan out the back of Jonkers. Bruce is wearing the infamous red bell-bottom trousers.

Walked 3 miles to trees & set rabbit traps. On returning we had a good meal & a shower followed by a dozen of S.A. beer. Played cards, sang songs & got generally pissed.

Sun. 8/9/68. – Arose at 7am (disgusting) to put old section car on train – then back to bed. Got up late – brunched – out to the traps – 5 out of 8 traps – not bad, but all pretty small. Polished off two remaining bottles – did rabbits & spent rest of afternoon, lying in the sun, washing, preparing stew etc. Had rabbit for tea – beautiful & spent evening playing Rummy – Bruce letter writing. My turn with the blankets.

Mon. 9/9/68. – Worked terribly hard for a Mon. – Read Snowman set traps with spud peelings. Trouble with section car – magneto – just got back before train/bus. Completed a 7 page letter to Sh.B., & 8 pages to Swinny. Bruce & Col spent the evening in a farting contest. Col retired; the victor by 8 farts! Did not enter myself – something wrong with the system – no farts.
EXTRA:– Observed the Snowman actually doing some packing.
Tues 10/9/68 – Another hard day packing – (very hot) Short evening of cards. Bruce stood out. Big event really. Had tea at Col's.
Wed 11/9/68 Raining! Short morning's work. Fellas played cards while Bruce writes letter to Irish. Pete recieves letter from Mandy (exit Peter). New arrival (Quien the Eskimo). Evening spent with cards & Bok beer.

A diary entry by the author and his mate, Pete.

Out in the open, where the mulga grows;
Two lads went "fettlin.", The Nullabor they chose.

Bruce & Pete, their names decried;
Aged twenty-one, or so they lied.

Out on the line, from morn till night;
They slaved for the Commonwealth, with all their might.

The Ganger, you know called himself Pete;
Who's remarkable pot equalled his feet.

A grumpy old b---- fully was he;
One night he came over & ruined our tea.

These lads, they travelled from Vic to West,
To see Australia, at it's best and the rest.

Augusta's the place that decided there fate;
'Cos to eat or not was the heated debate.

So employment they found without further ado;
To a place called "O'Malley" where people are few.

We were here a few days - still learning the ropes
When along came two more - stupid dopes.

A poem by Pete and Bruce.

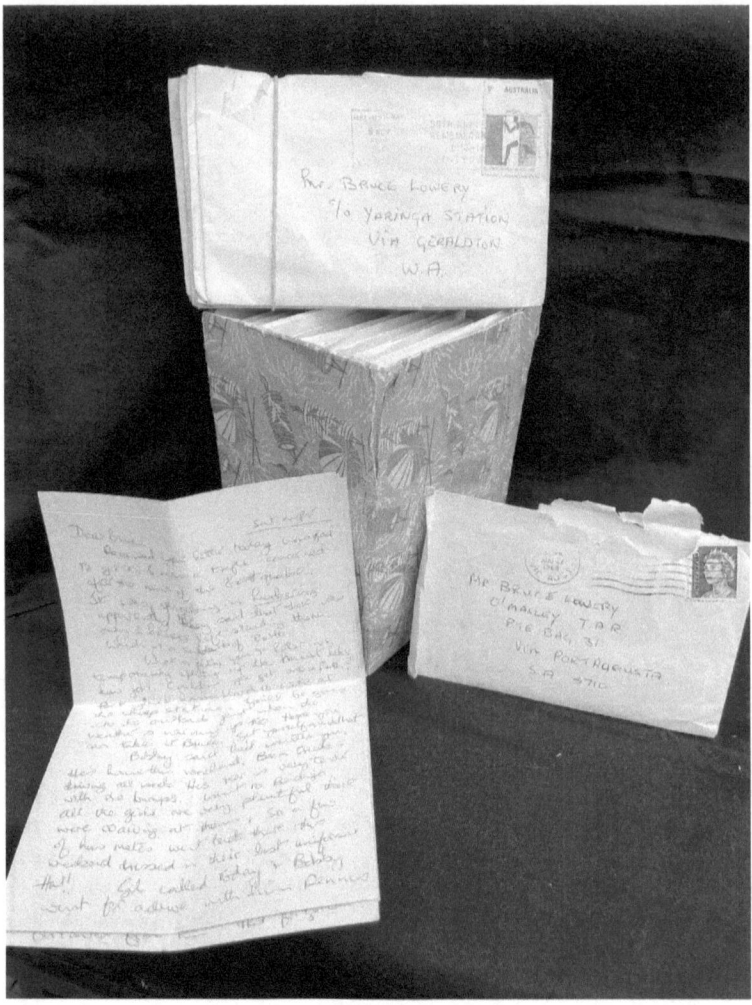

Some of the letters sent to Bruce during his travels, all of which have been kept in the box in the picture since '68. This was the very same box that the Robertson Bus Company used to return Bruce's camera whilst at Yaringa after he left it behind on the bus during the journey north.

9

YARINGA

Bob and I rose at 5am and showered. We grabbed our bags and a couple of packets of sandwiches that Ma Jonker had prepared for us the night before. As we headed out the door Pete suddenly appeared, having set his alarm specially to say farewell. We embraced quickly, wishing each other all the best before Bob and I suddenly found ourselves inside the pre-ordered cab that was winging it's way to the Perth Bus Depot. I looked at my bus ticket to make sure we were on time. It had been issued by the Robertson Bus Service and yes, it was to depart at 6am precisely. We were going to be spot on time.

As soon as we arrived at the depot, we hopped aboard our allotted bus with about a dozen or so other passengers, most of whom seemed a bit subdued. 'I guess it is fairly early in the day,' I said.

'Maybe they're sad because they're leaving the big smoke and heading off to woop woop,' reasoned Bob.

'No sense of adventure,' I agreed.

We kept ourselves entertained by telling each other pathetic jokes. After about two hours, the bus pulled into a pretty little fishing town named Lancelin for a ten-minute leg stretch and an opportunity for the passengers to buy a coffee, but then took off punctually on the highway heading north. The countryside seemed to be mainly made up of well cultivated wheat farms.

We rolled into Geraldton at around 11am, with the bus driver advising that if we needed to buy something for lunch, this was the last opportunity. We'd be stopping for half an hour precisely. Keeping our sandwiches for later in the day, Bob and I grabbed a couple of pies each and ate them on the spot. We then spent the remaining fifteen minutes poking around the place. It seemed like a nice country town, complete with a large seaport.

As the bus ground it's way north along the highway, we noticed the vegetation becoming sparser and drier. As the passing traffic became more and more scarce, we realised that Yaringa was going to be more than a little isolated. About mid-afternoon Bob went up to the driver to remind him that we wanted to get off the bus at Yaringa Sheep Station.

'What did he say mate?' I asked Bob as he returned to our seat.

'He said, what the fuck are you going there for?' 'It's in the middle of nowhere.'

It must have been about 4 o 'clock, when the bus finally ground to a halt on the side of the road.

'Here's your stop fellas,' yelled the driver over his shoulder.

Bob and I looked out the window, and then stared at each other. There were no buildings in sight – nor even a bus stop. We scrambled to get our things together. Nine hours on a bus had left us in a slightly comatose state and this sudden call for action had us floundering around like a couple of confused wombats.

'But where do we know where to go from here?' asked Bob.

The driver shrugged. Not his problem.

After we alighted, the bus rumbled off, gathering more and

more speed until it became a mere spec on the horizon. A little way ahead was a dirt road heading off to the right. As we walked up to it, we could see a small sign perched on a thin stick. It read Yaringa, with a small arrow pointing up the dusty road.

'Here we go mate,' said Bob without much enthusiasm, as we began to trudge along carrying our swags. The vegetation was stunted and all of it appeared to be covered with thorns. What the hell did the sheep eat?

After about half an hour of walking, a group of buildings came into view. We opened the station gate and walked along the long driveway until we reached the homestead front door. Bob knocked on it loudly. A middle-aged woman opened the door, poked her head out and said in a matter-of-fact voice, 'What can I do for you?'

A knock on the door of this extremely remote homestead can't have been all that frequent, so I'm not sure what or who she was expecting, but Bob rose to the occasion by enthusiastically announcing that we were the two new station hands, in a manner that inferred that *we* were their long-awaited saviours.

'Well, all workers have to enter via the tradesman's entrance,' said the thin woman with the utmost seriousness, pointing in the direction we were expected to head. With that she shut the door firmly in our faces.

Slightly taken aback, Bob and I wandered towards the rear of the homestead and knocked again on the back door. The same woman appeared once again.

'You'll be the new Jackaroo's then,' she announced confidently. 'My name is Mrs Baines. Is it Bob and Bruce then?'

As we nodded our agreement, Mrs Baines led us to a weather board clad bungalow situated at the rear of the homestead, advising that this was to be our quarters and that dinner would be served in a room just off the back veranda of the main homestead at 6.30 sharp. She then left us to our own devices.

'What a fucking welcome,' observed Bob, as soon as Mrs Baines was out of earshot.

'It was the genuine warmth and conviviality that got me Bob,' I joked sarcastically.

The room had two single beds covered with faded chenille bedspreads of indeterminate colour. There were two wooden bedside tables, two rough wooden wardrobes and two animal skins rugs on the floor. At the back of the room was a rudimentary bathroom. Feeling very thirsty, I grabbed a tin mug and filled it with water from the bathroom tap. Raising it to my mouth, I gulped down a large mouthful, before spitting it out violently.

'It tastes like shit,' I shouted. 'Ya silly bastard,' laughed Bob. 'It'll be bore water. Ya can't drink that stuff.'

After my time in O'Malley, I should have realised…

As we unpacked our meagre belongings, I quickly became aware that something was missing.

'Bugger,' I said. 'My camera has either dropped out of my bag, or I've left the bloody thing on the bus. I'm going to walk back to where the bus dropped us off to see if I can find it.'

I walked back slowly through the gate and down the road to the highway feeling really pissed off. I badly wanted to capture some images of this part of my travels, particularly since I had missed my chance in O'Malley.

I reached the spot where we got off the bus and was closely scanning the ground in the immediate vicinity, when suddenly I saw something very familiar folded up, and lying on the roadside. No camera but there in all their glory, and in all their isolation, were some genuine Australian legal tender bank notes.

I swooped on them, quickly counting out the value.

'You bloody beauty! Twenty-five fucking dollars,' I exclaimed.

The odds of finding the money in that remote location were

so low. We were at least 60 miles from the nearest neighbour, a hundred miles or more from the nearest roadhouse, and the bus would probably stop here no more than three or four times a year, when new workers arrived at, or departed from Yaringa. The find was nothing short of a miracle and a most welcome one, but it didn't alter the fact that my camera was nowhere to be seen.

I made it back to the Yaringa homestead just in time to wash my hands and head into our allocated dining area with Bob.

Two men greeted us. One was tall, thin and probably aged in his late forties. The other guy would have been in his mid-twenties, and about the same height as myself (a Collingwood six footer). Both were deeply tanned.

The older guy spoke first. 'I'm the manager of Yaringa, and you blokes can call me Mr Baines. What I say goes,' he announced in an unnecessarily forceful manner. 'This here is the owner's son Brian,' he added, looking over to the younger man, who smiled, said welcome and stuck out his hand.

Mr Baines then condescended to also stick out his mitt. 'This room is your dining area. We eat through there, so knock on the door if you need anything.'

There was to be no misunderstanding about the pecking order at Yaringa. We were staff, they were the bosses, and never the twain shall meet. I also realised at that moment that it was an undisputed fact that Mrs Baines was the person in the marriage with the outgoing personality; in relative terms, that is.

When it was served, the meal wasn't too bad. It consisted of lamb, potatoes and three veg, followed by tinned peaches and custard. Everything was on the bland side, but our plates were piled high, much to our relief. Hard outdoor yakka always produced huge appetites, so we knew that we would be needing plenty of good tucker each day.

It was starting to get dark as we finished our meals. I walked over to the adjacent room and knocked on the door as instructed.

'Where might I get a drink of water from later if I get thirsty?' I asked, still thinking of the bloody awful taste of bore water in my mouth.

'There's a tin mug for each of you in your room, and a large rainwater tank between the house and your quarters,' advised Mr Baines. 'Breakfast is served in the same room at 7am on Sundays, but always at 6am sharp every other day of the week.'

'What a ripsnorter,' said Bob cynically as we returned to our dismal sleeping quarters.

'A whole one-hour sleep in tomorrow, mate,' he grinned.

I merely grunted, then began a letter to the Robertson Bus Services about my missing camera. Bob was already in bed snoring when I took my tin mug outside to stride towards the big rainwater tank. On my way I noticed that the homestead was already in complete darkness.

'Early to bed makes a man...' I mumbled to myself, turning on the rainwater tank tap. Not a single frigging drop. 'Guess I'll have to go thirsty,' I muttered, as I walked back to tuck myself into my new cot.

THE NEXT MORNING Bob rose before me, farting, belching and scratching himself awake.

'Not a pretty sight,' I thought to myself,' but one I suppose I'd better get used to.'

As I was having a lukewarm shower, I realised how hard the bore water really was in this part of Australia. Try as I might, I could not get anything even resembling a lather from my cake of sunlight soap. Afterwards my hair dried so hard, it was as good as impossible to run a comb through it.

Breakfast consisted of Corn Flakes or Corn Flakes, backed

up with as much toast as we could eat, and all washed down with great steaming mugs of tea. Afterwards Brian joined us, offering to give us a 'cook's tour' of the place. When he heard about the empty rainwater tank, he apologised.

'That's why we have another six large tanks,' he said. 'We haven't had any rain to speak of for at least six months.'

Brian then took us to an area behind a large shed some distance from the homestead, where there was a row of about eight kennels. Outside each kennel was a work dog attached to a long chain. There was a mixture of kelpies and kelpie crosses, and every one of them looked up expectantly, as we arrived. I walked over towards them with the intention of giving them a pat.

'No patting the dogs, mate,' said Brian firmly. 'They're working dogs, so don't fuss over them too much,' he added, walking over to a large outdoor Coolgardie Safe and taking out some bags of raw meat.

He then walked over to each dog, depositing large chunks on the ground in front of each kennel. The dogs wolfed it all down in no time.

Meanwhile Brian instructed me to fill the dog's bowls with bore water.

'They don't drink that awful stuff, do they?' I asked.

'As I said, it sometimes doesn't rain here for many months, so rainwater is really very precious. And anyway, they don't know any different,' he shrugged.

'So how big is Yaringa?' I asked Brian.

'Around 350,000 acres, give or take', he replied.

'And how many sheep do you stock?' I said, hoping that that I was giving the impression of showing considerable interest.

'Probably around 10,000, but it's hard to be precise'.

'Are you bloody fair dinkum?' said Bob in astonishment. 'That's only about one sheep to every 35 acres?'

'Yep,' replied Brian with certainty. 'With the rainfall we've had over the last ten years or so, the vegetation won't sustain many more'.

'So, you're the owner's son, are you?' queried Bob.

'Yeah, I finished uni a couple of years ago and Dad thought the experience up here would do me good,' he said. 'I've learnt a lot, but I won't stay here forever'.

'What about Mr Baines – what's he like?' I said, trying to weigh things up a bit.

'Hard as nails and been doing this type of work for yonks.'

We walked over to a shed that housed the station vehicles, which consisted of some pick-up trucks with utility type backs behind each cabin. There were several motorbikes as well. I noticed that all the necessary equipment to repair and replace tyres, plus many assorted tools were all neatly hanging in their correct spot on the wall of the shed. A petrol bowser stood outside.

'We have to be completely independent here,' said Brian. 'We get a delivery of food, mail and other essentials once a week only, and sometimes the truck can't get here at all. The petrol tank is filled every couple of months. But everything has to be hauled up from Perth, so it's all very expensive.'

Today being Sunday is the only day we take off work, but even then, if Mr Baines thinks it's necessary, we'll work that day too,' he said. 'But not today,' he added brightly. 'It's going to be pretty hot, so if you walk back down to the highway, cross over to a small roadway on the other side, it'll take you to a jetty jutting out into Shark Bay. Don't hang about in the water too long though,' he added with apparent seriousness. 'We get sea snakes hereabouts, and one bite from them it's curtains. In fact,' Brian added with evident relish, 'I've only heard of one bloke who survived when he was bitten on the thumb, and a mate chopped it off within seconds with his tomahawk. They say that that was the only thing that saved him.'

'Thanks,' replied Bob in disgust. 'But getting bitten on the bum by a bloody snake while I'm swimming is not within cooee of my idea of having fun.'

After lunch it really began to heat up.

'Shit Bob, it's hot as hell, and I'm damned well bored as bat shit,' I said. 'Let's at least take a walk down to the jetty for a saunter along the beach'.

'Okay,' replied Bob, but don't ask me to go anywhere near the fucking water'.

We found the jetty easily enough. Apparently, many years before, the wool from Yaringa had been picked up from the jetty by smaller vessels than the ones operating in the 60's. It was quite an icon, sitting there all weather beaten, with the bright blue backdrop of Shark Bay in the background. Naturally, once we arrived, after walking for 45 minutes, we were both hotter than ever.

'Bugger it,' I said. 'There can't be that many bloody snakes in there,' I said, stripping off all my clothes, and walking carefully along the old jetty boards. 'In for a penny,' I said loudly with false bravado.

'Don't do it,' yelled Bob, covering his eyes with both of his hands. 'Yoooou can't leave me here in this wilderness all on my own.'

'Geronimo,' was all I yelled, as I jumped off the side of the old wooden structure. I barely hit the water before I was struggling up the side of the jetty, full of exhilaration and terror. I had repeated this several times more before Bob's big naked frame was suddenly beside me on the jetty.

'I want you to know that there is nothing in my will for you if I die,' Bob yelled at me, before grabbing his wedding tackle in his cupped hands and plunging arse-first into the water, creating a minor tidal wave along the shoreline that had a fair chance of reaching Carnarvon.

We continued with these wild antics for another hour or so, without either of us receiving the expected fatal bite. Finally, we'd had enough. We dried quickly in the sun, dressed and then explored the shoreline, unsuccessfully looking for any interesting relics, before heading back to our new home for dinner.

10

CHASING JUMBUCK

'Wakey wakey Bruce,' bellowed Bob as he shook me awake before heading off to the outdoor dunny. 'Breakfast in 5.'

I rolled out of bed with a yawn, and then performed similar ablutions myself, before joining Bob in our private dining room. We were still ramming as much food as possible into our mouths, when we were interrupted by the unmistakable flat voice of Mr Baines emanating from the adjacent room.

'Five minutes you blokes – so look lively.'

I swallowed my tea, rushed back to our room to grab my new hat, before following Bob out into the yard.

Mr Baines was backing one of the large utility style trucks out from the large shed that we'd seen the day before. Brian suddenly appeared preceded by half a dozen eager and excited dogs. Without hesitation, they all jumped up onto the back of the truck, giving delighted little barks.

'Stop ya yapping,' instructed Mr Baines sternly, which had an immediate effect on the dogs.

They settled down and were panting loudly, with their alert eyes darting about.

'You two blokes can get in with the dogs,' said Mr Baines in his monotone voice.

Our backsides had barely reached the floor of the truck, before we were off at speed, with the hot air rushing around us. I took off my hat and held on to it tightly.

'First class ticket again,' yelled Bob, grinning like a Cheshire cat.

Brian was in the cabin with the boss. We drove at speed for a good 45 minutes along dry, dusty and corrugated tracks with Bob and I hanging on grimly to the sides of the truck taking everything in. There were wire fences on each side of the track and the vegetation barely changed from what had seen already. Thorny stunted bushes and trees, with no discernible sign of grass.

We finally stopped, and all jumped out of the truck behind the dogs.

'We're going to be herding sheep in a westerly direction,' said the boss authoritatively, waving and pointing his arms in the desired direction. 'The four of us will need to fan out, and let the dogs do their work, but you new blokes need to understand that sometimes you'll have to give the sheep some physical encouragement.'

Off we started at a run, gradually driving the sheep dotted about in front of us forward. Every now and then a roo or two would see us and bound away at speed. Mr Baines and Brian were occasionally giving the dogs some whistled and verbal instructions like 'come behind', or 'round 'em up', but the dogs seemed to instinctively know what to do anyway. If a sheep failed to move with sufficient energy, or attempted take off in the wrong direction, each dog would simply nip the woolly heels of each particularly obstinate sheep, which usually produced the desired effect.

It has to be said that sheep are not the most intelligent of animals. I tried to listen and watch the experts carefully while running, shooing, yelling and waving my arms about vigorously like a maniac, but there were times that the bloody sheep would want to run in the opposite direction. I seemed unable to persuade them. The darn dogs were having far greater success.

I decided to try to coordinate the canine activities to boost my efficiency. I was trying to imitate the calls made by my more experienced benefactors in a loud voice. Suddenly Mr Baines appeared beside me.

'Don't confuse the damn dogs,' he said to me menacingly. 'Each one of them is worth more than ten of you,' he added, before running off.

Somewhat chastened, I kept on herding the sheep in my own largely ineffectual style.

After a couple of hours of work, we eventually had a good three to four hundred sheep in front of us. Once herded together they tended to keep moving together, and without quite so much energetic persuasion from us, or the dogs. The fence lines ahead on each side of us were becoming closer together, which in turn bunched the sheep up even more closely. Finally, we had them all into a fairly large pen. Adjacent to the large pen was a smaller one with a metal gate leading from the bigger pen into the smaller one.

'You get a fire started, so we can have a cuppa with our smoko,' instructed Mr Baines, directing his gaze straight at me.

No problems at all, I thought, immediately scouting around for sufficient firewood. I'd had plenty of experience with this on the Nullarbor.

I soon started a nice bright little fire in a previously made rudimentary fireplace. The billy boiled quickly enough, so I threw in some tea leaves, and vigorously swung the billy around in large arc in the time-honoured tea making art of the bushman.

'Not a bad brew from a city slicker,' commented Mr Baines, as he passed around a biscuit tin. 'Reckon you can have that job regularly.'

That was my first compliment from my boss in the entire day.

I rolled a fag and sipped on my tea. I was under no disillusionment. I was very green when it came to working in the bush. Obviously, those in charge had difficult jobs. The Ganger at O'Malley had been terribly inconsistent, and quite deranged when drunk, but he knew the work intimately. Mr Baines also clearly knew the ropes inside out, and his coldness and blunt commands were intended to keep workers in their place, but he wasn't averse to saying something positive every once in a while.

Best to stay on the right side of this guy, I determined.

After smoko, Bob and I were told to jump into the large pen with the sheep, and to herd them towards the small gate leading to either the smaller pen, or the outside area. The boss stood on the fence railing, opening and shutting the gate in order to send some sheep into the pen and the others outside to relative freedom. Finally, we had around 100 sheep in the smaller pen.

'These are the lambs that we need to mark,' said Mr Baines. 'So, you two now need to jump into the small pen with them'.

'There are some of these buggers who aren't lambs,' pointed out Bob, jumping inside the pen with the frankly terrified sheep.

'Yep,' replied the boss. 'We always miss a few each year, so there's probably a sprinkling of two- and three-year old's in there too,' he added, standing with Brian behind a small section of the pen fence that was noticeably lower.

'Now each of you pick up a lamb by the hind legs with his back against your belly and bring them over here'.

I picked up a rather hefty sized sheep and plonked it down with its arse resting on the lower railing in front of the boss. He set to work immediately by clipping quite large chunks out of sheep's ear with a device that looked, for all the world, like pinking shears.

'Shit, that would've hurt the poor bugger,' I thought, but worse was to come.

'Now hold the beast tight,' the boss said as he placed what looked like a thick elastic band on yet another handheld device, which, when he squeezed the handles together, opened up the rubber band into a wider circle. He then opened up the sheep's legs wide and slipped the ring around the base of his testicles. Mr Baines then grabbed a sharp knife and cut off the sheep's tail with one quick blow. Blood spurted into the air, with much of it hitting my face and shirt.

'This to reduce the chances of the sheep getting blowfly', he explained.

It was hard to see how blowfly could be less painful than what I'd just witnessed, but I assumed it had to be.

Having thrown the tail away, the boss then took a brush out of a nearby pail that was filled with a white disinfectant fluid and sloshed the wet stuff around the sheep's nether regions. He then helped the poor woolly one out of my arms, releasing it to the area outside the pen. It ran off squealing towards the other mature sheep.

'Don't worry,' said the boss. 'Most of them won't need the ring, because they'll be ladies.'

I heard some loud squawking noises gathering in volume. I looked up and saw a murder of crows gathering around us in the small trees and bushes.

'They're just waiting for the tails,' said the boss. 'I hate those damn birds. They've been known to take the eyes out of live lambs,' he added.

'Why don't you shoot a few?' I asked, trying to keep hold the next victim tightly.

'By the time I got my gun out of the truck, they would all

have disappeared,' replied Mr Baines as he cut off another tail with a swift blow of his knife.

'Oh,' I said, trying to dodge the spurt of crimson coloured blood.

'They're the most cunning creatures out here. Next sheep, please'.

Once we finished, Bob and I wandered over to the canvas water bags strapped to the front of the truck. I splashed some of the contents over my face and arms to wash off the congealed sheep blood.

'Go easy on the water,' shouted the boss. 'It's for drinking'. I looked over at Bob to see him clearly mouth the words 'fuck 'em'.

I re-started the fire and soon had the billy boiling again. The late lunch of large mutton sandwiches went down well with a mug of tea. We spent the rest of the day checking out bores on the property. The familiar looking steel windmills spun in the wind, continually pumping up water from deep underground. Mr Baines made some adjustments and took notes about any repairs needed. At least the less strenuous activities in the afternoon gave Bob and I some opportunity to recover from the long mornings' exertions. Regardless, we were in bed not long after dinner that night.

The next day was pretty much a repeat of the day before. Just the location was different. The dogs worked just as impressively, never slowing and always persistent. I continued to exert a great deal of energy into the exercise and thought that I was improving. I was anticipating each sheep's movement a good deal better and kept most moving along nicely.

Bob seemed to be having a ball, referring to the sheep around him with names like Boofhead, Dipstick, Drongo, Piker and Fruit Loop. He had an endless supply of derogatory terms.

Somehow, his use of them seemed to indeed have the desired effect on his woolly subjects.

At one point I came across a huge sheep, lying in the relative shade of a small scrubby tree. I tried mightily to lift it up onto its legs, but it simply refused to budge. It truly was a large beast. I called out to Mr Baines, who ran over.

'This one won't move,' I explained. 'It seems too fat.'

'Nah, it's missed several shearing years, so it's got too much wool, which is slowing it down,' replied the boss. 'Just leave it.'

Rather taken aback, I began to splutter 'But we can't......'

'Just leave it,' repeated the boss, running off and yelling to the dogs.

'No room for compassion out here,' I thought reluctantly to myself, leaving the poor panting animal to die a long-drawn-out death.

The activity in the pens was also similar to the day before, with what seemed to be the same 'flamin' crows' arriving for their sheep tail feeds. My efforts to avoid the blood spurts to the face only improved marginally. It was difficult to dodge the sudden upward gushes, while you were trying hold on to a horrified sheep that was understandably wriggling with sheer terror.

During the smoko and lunch breaks my fire and tea making skills continued to improve, but the compliments from the day before were not repeated. It seemed that mutton sandwiches were 'de rigueur' out here at Yaringa. I didn't think I'd tire of them.

At the end of the day's work, the dogs, Bob and I jumped into the back of the truck. The two humans quite exhausted, the dogs less so. We hadn't even sat down when the truck revved up and took off at speed. I failed to hang on to my new hat, so it unexpectedly sailed off my head, disappearing in a large cloud of dust.

I thumped on the cabin roof yelling 'I've lost my hat, please stop.' There was no response from the two blokes in the cabin. They stared straight ahead with the truck accelerating to an even greater speed.

'Well, I'll be fucked,' I said to Bob. 'The bloody bastards.

When we arrived back at the homestead, I jumped down, and fronted Mr Baines. 'Didn't you hear me yell that my hat had blown off?' I said with considerable annoyance in my voice.

'Too bad,' replied the boss in his flat unemotional voice. 'It's not my fault if the boy can't hold on to his hat,' he added over his shoulder as he walked away towards the house. I was left with my mouth open, staring after him.

'C'mon,' said Bob. 'Let's clean up for dinner.'

I was rather dispiritedly eating my evening meal that night when Mr Baines appeared.

'It's hot and thirsty work out there each day boys,' he said. 'Would you like a bottle of beer each night with your meals?'

Would we bloody ever!

He returned a short while later with *two* cold large, long neck bottles of Emu Bitter with the tops removed, and two seven-ounce beer glasses.

'Thanks a million,' enthused Bob.

I was shaken out of my previously sullen attitude.

'I'll make sure you get these every night with your dinner,' the boss added.

Whilst the initiative was most agreeable, this man was proving to be quite an enigma. Was he trying to say sorry, or was something else happening here?

'He's a bloody top bloke,' was all my mate Bob had to say.

It was the usual start to a day. Bob's early morning flatulence knew no bounds and his scrotum scratching had to be seen to be believed. However, it had to be admitted that his sharp wit and crazy humour more than made up for his post-dawn bodily malfunctions. On balance, he wasn't such a bad mate to have an adventure with.

As Bob stuffed his fourth slice of toast in his mouth, and me my third (I never could keep up with him in the eating stakes), Mr Baines looked around the corner into the staff eating quarters.

'More marking again today boys, so look lively.'

Within minutes we were charging off into the early morning light to an entirely new location. The dogs jumped and bounded around the confined area in the back of the truck, often grabbing parts of our clothes with their teeth in agitated excitement. It was crystal clear that they *loved* this work, and that the anticipation was almost too much for them to bear.

As we began our now familiar act of sheep herding, I started to take more notice of our surroundings. Apart from the ever-present roos there was also the occasional emu, but both quickly moved away from our activities at speed. Also, every now and then I'd spot a herd of goats. There were usually about a dozen or more nannies and young bucks, but there was always a large male billy out in front leading the way, usually complete with two impressively twirling horns majestically jutting out from his head. They also always veered away from us, making sure they didn't get caught up in the human/dog/sheep circus making its way unceremoniously through the West Australian bush.

'I had no idea that there would be so many goats out here,' I said to Brian at smoko that morning.

'Yeah, Europeans introduced them into the bush, and they thrive out here,' he responded. 'They're now in plague proportions, so we often go out on a shooting spree to cull them back.'

'What other introduced species are out here, apart from the obvious ones like rabbits and foxes?'

'It's not unusual to come across camels and believe it or not dogs and cats also become totally wild and untamed out here. We shoot those bastards on sight because they do untold damage to the sheep as well as many of the native species.'

There's a whole lot of killing out here, I thought to myself as I inhaled some smoke from my hand-rolled fag and reached for my mug of tea.

True to his word, Mr Baines brought out two more long neck bottles of Emu Bitter for us to enjoy with our meals again that night. It certainly made for a much more enjoyable end to a hard day's work. Afterwards I settled down to write letters to Trish, Pete and the folks, in order to catch the mail truck that was scheduled for the following Friday.

It didn't seem possible, but the next day started out even hotter than the previous ones. We continued our sheep chasing, penning, lifting and disfiguring activities with gay abandon. The number of two- and three-year-old so-called lambs seemed to be even greater in number, making Bob and my task ever more strenuous.

'No point in complaining,' said Bob during that morning's smoko. 'Some people have to pay to go a gym to get this much heavyweight lifting.'

'Yeah, but their gym equipment doesn't piss and bleed all over them,' I retorted.

'Fair point,' Bob conceded.

That evening we showered as usual, but it was still so hot that Bob and I both went to dinner without wearing a top. Mrs Baines entered our dining area carrying two of our usual steaming plates of mutton and three veg. She suddenly stopped in her tracks as though she'd been shot with a .303 bullet and stared with utter astonishment at her two bare chested diners.

'John,' she called out in a loud and obviously agitated voice.

'You had better come and deal with this,' she shouted, still holding on to our meals.

Mr Baines arrived at speed, almost skidding to a halt and hissed: 'Get back to your room, and dress yourselves properly for dinner.'

Once we had each donned a ragged and none too clean shirt (read, sheep-blood encrusted) and returned to our dining room, Mr Baines explained forcefully that standards must be maintained at all times at Yaringa. It was mandatory that we always dressed properly for dinner. Our meal and beer were then provided to each of us without further comment.

'Well fuck me,' was all Bob could whisper to me in wide eyed wonder, once our two instructors had left the room.

I just shook my head.

WE ARRIVED BACK from another strenuous day of enforcing utter misery upon our woolly subordinates to find that the mail truck had indeed arrived earlier in the day, and that I had two newsy letters from my folks.

My dear mum had written:

> I received the letter that you wrote before leaving Perth today and was very glad. I was a trifle concerned when I heard about the earthquake in Meckering. What a pity you and Peter are temporarily splitting up. I hope that your new mate Bob is a nice, friendly, reliable chap. I suppose that you will have to work very hard at the sheep station and will be in the outback just when the

weather is warming up. Hope you can take it Bruce. Get yourself a hat.

Next, I read a letter from dad.

So, you're a Jackaroo now. Gee you sure are seeing life!

What I'm going to write now, I want you to accept as a 'buddy' talk son. Last night we had a visit from Trish's father. It would seem that between them, they are having arguments in their home. He would like you to stop writing letters to Trish for a while as he believes it would help their family matters, and give her an opportunity to find different interests, other than boys. Please do as he asks, son. This is not meant to be a lecture. As I've said to you before, you are leadership material, and have determination and guts. Apply them, and you will see how kind God is.

So how about 'shining', and sending us some good newsy letters about your adventures? Go to it with all your heart and make us proud of you.

Dad's letter struck me like a thunderbolt. Stop writing to Trish? Fuck that!

After eating my meal in silence, I walked outside to think about the request from my father. I sat down beside the dogs. They were quiet and seemed to sense my distress. I sat staring at the setting sun and thought hard.

Being more isolated again was giving me more time to think about Trish, and I felt that my love for her was, if anything, even stronger than before. Perhaps the old adage that 'absence makes the heart grow fonder' was at play here.

I decided that I was not going to let others dictate that our relationship should end. If Trish herself wanted me to cease writing, I would do so immediately, but until then I would continue to write to her covertly, via our friends.

As we drove out to a new sheep herding location at speed the next morning, the truck suddenly braked to a halt. Bob and I looked over to see a damaged section of the fence wrapped around a still struggling emu. The poor bird had obviously hit the wire at top running speed, quickly and hopelessly entangling itself in the metal strands.

The boss jumped out of the truck cabin and dispatched the large bird by swiftly cutting its neck with his ever-present knife.

'Damn thing,' he cursed loudly towards the still twitching carcass.

'There's another bloody fence to fix'.

We drove on without another word being spoken. No compassion for the dead bird whatsoever. There was just anger at the extra work that had been created.

After we arrived back at the homestead that afternoon, the boss turned to Brian.

'Take these two blokes and show them how we slaughter a sheep for the kitchen Brian,' he said, before striding off towards the house.

Bob and I, together with the full pack of dogs, dutifully followed Brian to a small paddock containing three of four mature aged sheep. Brian strode up to one and forced it off its feet to lie on its side on the ground. He quickly produced some strong twine from his pocket and tied the by then terrified sheep's front and back legs.

'Pick her up lads and carry her over to the far corner of the paddock.' Bob and I grunted our agreement, eventually placing the wildly struggling animal on its back on a crude wooden structure not unlike a wood cutting horse.

The dogs were all excitedly following hard on our heels.

'The most important thing about slaughtering,' emphasised Brian. 'Is to minimize the suffering of the creature'.

He produced his knife, pulled the poor sheep's head back and plunged the long blade into its neck.

'You have to go in quickly and cut the spinal cord,' said Brian as he expertly cut through to the base of the neck, and then completed the slitting of the sheep's throat while the beasts' legs continued to kick spasmodically. Blood gushed out onto the ground underneath the wooden structure where the dogs had been waiting with keen anticipation. They began to lick up the blood with relish.

'That's fucking disgusting,' said Bob vehemently, pointing to the dog's activities. 'Good nourishment for them,' replied Brian. 'Turn your stomach, does it?' he added with a smirk.

'Nah,' said Bob. 'The sheep's carked it now, and any way I've got the strongest stomach this side of the black stump'.

I wasn't so convinced by Bob's statement. He looked a bit green around the gills to me. 'I bet you wouldn't lick up a mouthful,' goaded Brian, fortunately directing his gaze at my mate and not me.

'What would you pay me if I did?' replied Bob without blinking.

'An extra bottle of beer with dinner, but you have to swallow the mouthful of blood, dirt and dog saliva too,' said Brian evenly.

'No problem,' came the unequivocal reply from Bob.

Now I'm not a squeamish bloke generally, but my stomach certainly turned a couple revolutions as my buddy got down on his hands and knees and commenced his ghastly task, while pushing the dogs to one side with his beefy arm, much to their consternation. After making some frankly sickening licking and slurping noises Bob finally emerged from the ground grinning triumphantly and making a great show of swallowing hard. Christ! He hadn't been joking when he told me he was hard man!

At dinner that night, Bob was duly served up his extra bottle of amber fluid. He made a great show of enjoying it, making loud belching sounds in my general direction.

When we had finally retired to bed, I was just nodding off when an obscenely loud explosive sound rent the air from the direction of Bob's bed.

'Sorry old chap,' said my bloated mate in a poor attempt at a mock Etonian accent. 'Must have been something I ate'.

'Go to bloody sleep Bob,' I mumbled as I rolled over.

I JOINED Bob for the luxury of a late start Sunday morning breakfast. We were both tired from the week's exertions, so the conversation was a bit stunted. Bob went back to bed afterwards while I stuck my head in a book while sitting on the shady veranda. There was no sign of the upper echelon folk, save for the Mrs bringing us breakfast earlier.

After lunch, I excused myself by saying that I was going for a bit of a walk. Bob was proving to be a great mate as I had expected but living and working together 24/7 was a lot to ask of any relationship.

I made my way down to the old wharf and sat down in complete solitude. The only sounds were the squawking of seabirds and the lapping of the waves. I stared out at Shark Bay through to the extreme vastness of the Indian Ocean. I had never been so completely isolated in my life.

The Nullarbor came a close second, but I was always in close proximity to Pete and the other fettlers while I was there. This moment of solitude gave me the first opportunity since travelling to contemplate things without distractions. What would the future bring? Would this travel bug take over my life entirely? It was certainly proving to be addictive. But then there was my aching heart from my enforced separation with Trish. I was aware of the saying that 'the first cut is the deepest' and knew instinctively that this was without doubt the case with the two of us.

The all-consuming activities of the past few months had, for the most part, kept my emotions in check, but now they welled up threatening to overwhelm me once more. I continued to stare at the ocean of deep blue. A lump formed in my throat. My eyes blinked back salty tears. I knew my love for Trish still ran very deep.

I eventually roused myself and slowly began my slow walk along that totally isolated coastline breathing in the sea smells. I began to hum the tune to Donovon's 'Catch the Wind' to myself. It fully captured my feelings of loss and longing and refused to leave my brain as I tramped along the sand.

I eventually returned to the Yaringa homestead in time for dinner. I'd completely lost track of time. It turned out I'd been away with my thoughts for over four hours, with that beautiful song almost continually running around in my head and playing with my emotions. The afternoon had been profoundly moving.

'Where ya been, ginger nuts?' Bob's big voice boomed out as I walked onto the homestead veranda. 'Only the blackfellas are s'posed to go walkabout up here mate,' he continued.' We were about to send out a search party. No doubt you've been dreaming about your sheila back home, ya silly dickhead'.

I grinned back at my big mate. His accurate but coarse summary of my day had abruptly brought me back to earth, which was precisely where I needed to be.

As we finished our start of the working week Monday breakfast, Mr Baines strode into our dining area. 'Change of activities today you blokes,' he announced. 'We're going to be doing some burning off, so wear a long sleeved shirt and no shorts.'

Burning off? What the hell did that mean?

Bob and I had the back of the truck to ourselves as we sped off along a dusty track. The dogs had been left behind for the first time on a working day since we had arrived. Finally, we stopped at an area that looked the same as everywhere else I'd seen at Yaringa.

'The weather is perfect for the next few days for us to burn off some of this scrub,' said the boss authoritatively, as he and Brian grabbed four cans of diesel fuel, and some old newspapers from a large metal box on the back of the truck and passing the same over to us. My jaw dropped. I had lived most of my life in the Dandenong Ranges in Victoria, where we spent our summers on high alert for bushfires that had the potential to wipe out whole communities.

'Isn't this a bit dangerous?' I ventured.

'Just do as you're told,' came the prickly reply.

As instructed, we split up over a wide area, pulled branches off the stunted trees and bushes and piled them high. We then poured a small amount of diesel over the carefully laid bits of newspaper within, lit them and stood back. Whoosh. The flames caught on quickly in the dry atmosphere.

I watched on nervously, but unlike a fire in the Victorian bush, the fire burned slowly yet steadily through the scrub. We repeated this exercise in different locations throughout the morning, but always going back to check the progress of each burn. It was hot work and we kept choking back on the smoke-filled air.

During the lunch break, I apologised for having the temerity to question the boss's commands but asked again why it was necessary to burn the bush.

'I've learnt a few things over the years about managing the land,' explained Mr Baines. This idea was passed on to me by some Aboriginal elders,' he continued. 'Not all station owners do it, but in my opinion those black guys know what they're talking about. It's a regenerative process for the bush out here'.

I sat mulling the information over. It was difficult to accept after being taught about the terrifying threat of bushfires all my life. Nevertheless, out here in this dry arid country, with its sparse vegetation, the fires all seemed to be quite under control, and unlikely to pose any problems. Any animals in the vicinity seemed to scurry and bound away from the danger. It was all very interesting, but still rather vexing.

11

NO BLUDGIN'

We took off without the dogs to yet another part of the vast Yaringa station. Our job was to again carry out the now familiar exercise of burning the West Australian bush. It was hot and thirsty work and we regularly trotted back to the truck to swallow vast quantities of water from the canvas bags hanging from the front of the vehicle. Amazingly, these canvas bags kept many litres of water perfectly cool through the process of evaporation. Another fantastic invention that made working in the hot Australian outback tolerable.

As we were driving back to the homestead at the end of another arduous day, Bob and I spotted a most surprising sight. Either side of the track there were solid wire fences, and up ahead there was a mother emu running in front of the truck with her young chick running hard behind, trying to keep up. They were both moving at an amazingly high speed as they tried to outrun our truck.

As we drew closer, both birds moved to one side of the track. Bob yelled to Brian to slow down. As we drew level with the young chick, Bob leaned over the side of the truck, grasped the smaller bird by its long neck with his large paw of a hand, and lifted its whole body off the ground. I watched in total amazement as the younger birds' legs continued with same running motion in mid-air, without actually touching the ground. All four workers laughed spontaneously at this incredible sight. Bob in particular seemed to be highly delighted, his whole body heaving with mirth. Fortunately, he regained sufficient control of himself to successfully lower the chick carefully back to the ground, where the bird continued to run after its mother as if nothing had happened.

That night over dinner, Bob again returned to the story of the running emus. 'What a bloody bottler,' laughed Bob. 'Did you see the buggers' legs still going like the clappers in mid-air when I lifted him up?'

'I'm not sure that the emu appreciated the joke quite as much as you,' I said a bit caustically. 'Apart from the birds bruised neck, you may have dropped it under the truck's wheels, and killed it.'

'Ah, pull your bloody head in Lowery,' said Bob. 'It was only a fucking joke.'

Bob's eyes narrowed, and he became unusually serious. 'You don't get it yet do you mate? Not only are the emu's expendable out here, but so is everything else that breathes. The sheep, the dogs, you, me. Everything is expendable'.

It seemed that the callous approach to life in northwest Australia was contagious, or was I still too damned soft? Certainly, I'd just experienced Bob's more assertive side for the first time. His view on life in the Australian bush was certainly quite a bleak one.

AS WE BEGAN a new workday the dogs rejoiced as they were released from their prolonged confinement over the past few days. They barked and jumped onto the waiting truck. Even after the truck took off speedily, they kept bounding from one side to the other without regard to Bob and I. We grinned at each other, and then at the dogs.

'Tally Ho,' bellowed Bob as he bent forward into the onrushing hot air, his black matted hair barely moving due to constant washing in hard bore water.

Away from the choking smoke of the previous two days, our exhilaration continued throughout the morning as we herded the woolly ones. Even the stupidity and stubbornness of the dumb sheep that day didn't interfere with our happiness. A happy dog equals a happy human, and you can multiply that many times over when you are with a number of hard-working canines.

As we sat munching our sandwiches and sipping our tea during the well-deserved lunch break, the conversation between Bob and I turned towards music and various performers. Bob wasn't as ardent as I was, but he was always happy to chat about matters other than work.

Mr Baines ignored the discussion completely whilst chewing on his food methodically, as if it was just another task for the day. However, Brian was listening in about the merits of The Who versus The Animals.

'I don't know much about the music world,' he said. 'But you, Bruce, seem to be almost obsessed about it'.

'You better believe it,' I replied. 'I'm missing it badly'.

'You should have said something before now,' replied Brian. 'I've got a transistor radio you can borrow occasionally if you want,' he continued.

'Yes please,' I breathed, hardly believing my ears.

That night after dinner, as promised, Brian offered me the precious electrical device.

'Of course, reception up here is terrible,' he apologised, 'but you can borrow it tonight, for what it's worth.'

I hurried to our sleeping quarters, climbed into bed, plugged the radio into the nearby power outlet, and twiddled with the dial. Brian was right. The reception was appalling. After much searching, I found Station 6KY, whose broadcast from Perth faded in and out to such a degree that at best I could discern 20 or 30 seconds at a time. Nevertheless, so deprived of anything with a tune for so long, I persisted, catching a few bars of a number of mainly familiar pop songs, and the occasional word or two from the disc jockey.

As I was just about slip into a deep sleep, the radio reception cleared momentarily, and I heard the distinctive sound of an organ being played slowly and building up in volume. Suddenly a slow but strong drumbeat joined the organ before a lead guitar began to wail. What the hell!

The music faded slightly before a gruff gravelly voice sang 'What would you do if I sang out of tune. Would you stand up and walk out on me'. The station reception faded to a buzz. I knew the lyrics of The Beatles song 'With a Little Help from My Friends', but this was something else altogether. I pressed my left ear up to the transistor radio willing the reception to return. Finally, it did. The gruff voice was now squealing with emotion.

I was completely transfixed until the music again faded away before returning with the announcer saying, 'That was the fabulous Joe C... He faded out again.

'Fuck,' I thought to myself. 'I don't even know the artist's full name.' I was awestruck by what I had just heard.

WE HADN'T TRAVELLED FAR the next morning when we came across another part of the fence line that was broken. It had been hit at speed by a large roo, who lay dead in the tangle of wire. There wasn't a lot left of poor bugger. Most of his flesh had been ripped off his bones.

'Dingoes,' said Brian knowingly. 'That would have been an easy kill for them'.

'More damn fences to repair,' muttered Mr Baines fiercely, making a note in his pad about the location.

It was only about 15 minutes later that we stopped again. Mr Baines leapt out of the truck cabin and kicked the obviously flat tyre.

'Brian, show these two blokes how to change this thing,' the boss said angrily as he strode off into the bush.

Brian showed us how to loosen the wheel bolts, place the jack carefully under the truck, raise it, and replace the wheel with a flat tyre with a good one. It was to be the first of many, many such wheel replacements. The rough country certainly took its toll on many things.

The bad start to the day caused us all to feel pretty darn flat, which was in sharp contrast to the atmosphere of the day before. The dogs retained their high level of enthusiasm and excellent work ethic as we began to herd the sheep once more. We had a lot to learn from our tail wagging buddies. My efforts to revive my flagging spirits were dashed when Brian asked for the return of his transistor so he could try to listen to some news that night. Bugger!

As breakfast ended the following day, I approached the boss's dining area. I'd run out of my Drum tobacco, and my need for a nicotine hit was becoming acute.

'Excuse me Mr Baines,' I began. 'Do you have any stock of tobacco that I could have on tick against my salary?'

The boss nodded and I felt awash with relief.

As we walked towards the truck the boss threw me a small yellow tin. Printed on the lid were the words 'Log Cabin – Flaked Gold Leaf Tobacco'. I prised open the lid so I could quickly roll a fag before the truck got going. Inside was the coarsest and driest tobacco I had ever seen. Either this was the way it was produced by the manufacturer, or the tin had been stored at Yaringa for who knows how long.

Beggars can't be choosers, I figured as I managed to roll my first smoke for the day. I got used to this rough brand of old weed surprisingly quickly – such was the level of my addiction.

The day consisted of repairing damaged fences. Bob and I dug the fence pole holes using a device called a fence post auger. It looked like a giant wine corkscrew. We were directed to various locations along the fence line by Brian, where we toiled under the hot sun. We drilled into the bone-dry soil, periodically removing the auger to knock out the soil before returning it the hole again to make it even deeper. Once the numerous holes had reached their desired depths, Brian or Mr Baines came and held a wooden fence pole in the hole, while Bob or I would fill in the hole, leaving the pole standing firmly upright. The wooden poles were augmented with numerous metal Y pickets placed every five metres away from the sturdier wooden ones. These were bashed into the soil with a sledgehammer. It was Brian and Mr Baines job to then thread through the new strands of wire and tightening the tension with a strange looking toggling device.

Fencing was as physically demanding as herding and marking sheep – but then again, every task out here was hard yakka.

'No chance of bludging a bit, even on a Saturday,' Bob ventured when Brian and the boss were out of earshot.

'Nope,' I agreed. 'We earn every darned cent of our pay up here'.

When we got back, I was given a some more mail that had arrived earlier in the day. The first one I opened was from Mum:

> We're keeping track with your travels on a map of Australia. Geoff and I put a cross at each stop you've made. P.S. Just a word of advice from an old 'un. Forget about Trish and enjoy your travels. This is something you'll have to look back on when you're an old man. Don't get witty over a girl again. You had 18 months of too much of that, so forget about her.

I chaffed against the words my mother had written about my relationship with Trish. It had obviously been well intended, but it was clear that there were aspects that she simply didn't understand.

The second letter from my old mate Gil certainly brightened me up a bit:

> Good to hear from you again. Hope that you're well and haven't put any rings on your own nuts (it could be a bit irritating). The station sounds like a good place to be. I might join you when I finish my welding course.

BOB and I gratefully slept the extra hour that the seventh day of the week allowed, only just making it to our dining room for the stipulated 7 am deadline for feeding. The conversation between Bob and I centred upon the merits of herding sheep on foot versus the possibilities of doing so on motorbikes when Brian suddenly appeared in the doorway.

'I was thinking about the fact that you guys were missing music so much,' he said. 'So, I thought you might come and join me in the homestead lounge room to listen to our music collection for a couple of hours. Say around 2 o'clock?'

'Yes please,' we said happily.

Even though Mrs Baines had excelled herself by producing an excellent mutton roast dinner for lunch with potatoes and three veg, 2 o'clock couldn't come quickly enough. My mind began wander. What musical treats would soon unfold?

Eventually Bob and I were invited through to the sanctified space beyond the servants' quarters, settling into a fairly large room replete with old fashioned lounge chairs and a sofa. In one corner sat a square box like structure on a small coffee table. My excitement mounted as Brian lifted the top off the box revealing a rudimentary record player. Rudimentary or not, if it played music, it was God's gift that afternoon.

Brian beamed as he picked up the grand total of five LP (long playing) records and passed them over to me.

'What'll we play first?' he said.

I looked at the records in my hands and glanced over to see Bob grinning from ear to ear with a merry twinkle in his eye (or was that a mocking smile?). Four of the five records were all by Slim Dusty with the fifth entitled 'The Greatest Hits of Mario Lanza', with the great man's chubby face beaming back at me.

Fuck me, I thought. Country music and opera were the only two genres of music that I don't much like, or even understand. I concealed my disappointment as well as I could and passed over one of Slim Dusty's best to Brian.

We listened to Slim sing hits like 'The Lights on the Hill', 'Cunnamulla Feller', 'Leave Him in the Long Yard', 'and 'Ringer from the Top End'. I had to admit that my previous distaste for Slim's work was diminishing by the minute. By the time we had listened to three of his albums I was quite enjoying myself. Bob too, had his toe tapping. It must be said that Slim had a pretty ordinary voice, but the lyrics were about the Australian outback I was experiencing, and the music itself was growing on me.

'How come you like Slim so much?' I asked Brian.

'Well, he's the only performer I know who regularly tours outback Australia. I've seen him perform several times, and it's always been in a small country town. People come from miles and miles to see him. He's very much loved in the bush,' Brian concluded.

'Hmmm', I thought to myself. 'Maybe I've underestimated the guy'.

Just then Mrs Baines strode into the room. 'I'd like to hear a few tracks from Mario please,' she said.

'Of course,' replied Brian.

We sat patiently listening to songs with titles like 'With a Song in my Heart', 'Arrivederci Roma', and 'Because Your Mine'. Eventually Mario reached deep into his repertoire and began to sing some distinctly operatic numbers. My eyes glazed over with boredom.

'Thank you, Brian,' said Mrs Baines eventually. 'I must get back to my chores now,' she said, leaving the room.

Out of the corner of my eye I saw Bob leave his comfortable chair and raise himself to his full height while clasping his massive paw like hands together in a manifestly plaintive manner. He took a deep breath and began to sing in a vaguely operatic manner. His flat monotone voice was suddenly being propelled at high volume throughout the room. The words were a strange concoction of Italian gibberish, except for the chorus, which was clear enough:

Bobs eyes rolled in his head impressively, and it had to be admitted that his hand gesticulations were near perfect. I couldn't take my eyes off him. Could this be Bob's perfect moment? The song finally reached its zenith, and my mate impressively drew the performance to its inevitable close with him wiping his brow with large but none too clean handkerchief and beaming at Brian and I. It was only then that I realised that Mrs Baines had returned to the room to see what the fuss was about. The look on her face indicated considerable distaste. Brian quickly ushered Bob and I back to our quarters with understandable haste.

NOTHING WAS SAID about the previous day's antics as we joined the dogs in the back of the truck the next morning, but the overall atmosphere was hardly bright and breezy. It was just the usual terse instructions delivered by Mr Baines without any apparent emotion. Both Bob and I sensibly decided to stay shtum.

There was no doubt that I was fitter than when I had arrived two weeks earlier. The work was still hard, but I was certainly coping better, despite the oppressive heat. The sheep were something else. At the best of times, they are a far from quick witted animal, but the buggers spent most of their days aimlessly wandering through the desolate landscape, often not seeing humans for months, or even years at a time. This made the sheep at Yaringa even more timorous, frightened, and stupid than usual. As we approached them with our dogs yapping, they were likely to run off in all the wrong directions, and sometimes, they would simply drop to the ground, and refuse to move. If vigorous nips from the dogs failed to get them moving, Bob or I would have to lift them up and shove them towards the desired location. Often this action had to be repeated many times with the same bloody sheep, giving rise to considerable frustration. Nevertheless, we eventually had our two hundred odd sheep herded into the waiting pens.

During the lunch break, Bob sat staring at the bleak landscape. 'Do ya reckon anyone has ever tried to measure a sheep's IQ?'

'Dunno,' I replied. 'Doesn't seem to be any point to the exercise.'

'Well. I'd like to know if there are any other similar sized animals that have smaller brains,' persisted Bob. 'Every bloody last one of them is a few sandwiches short of a picnic'.

I considered this for a while, while sipping on my second large mug of tea.

'In my experience most animals I know, are a good deal smarter,' I suggested. 'But I do know quite a few blokes with about the same intelligence as sheep'.

'Me too,' enthused Bob. 'I knew a drongo once who was completely obsessed with sex. Honestly, he was the original Root Rat, chasing females every second of the day'.

'Not too much wrong with that is there?'

'Well, he thought he was pretty smart until he was caught totally chockers by a certain lady's bikie lover. Hells Angel he was,' intoned Bob, shaking his head sadly.

'Jeepers,' I replied. 'What happened to him?'

'Let's just say he doesn't piss standing up anymore. Less brains than a sheep, that dickhead.'

My ability to judge the upward velocity of sheep blood when they had their tales cut off was improving, but only slightly. The problem was that a bloke had to pick up a sheep one way only in order for the marking process to take place, and you were always directly in the firing line when a sheep had good blood pressure. The strange thing was that both Brian and Mr Baines rarely found themselves similarly drenched with the red stuff. I worked it out that placing the sheep's butt on a slightly different angle helped considerably. However, my experimentation was suddenly cut short when I changed the angle too much and Mr Baines copped a face full. He certainly wasn't impressed. Bob thought it was darn funny, but I knew that I had earned yet another black mark with the boss.

As we were returning to the homestead late in the afternoon the ute slowed to a halt. 'Come on Lowery, get a fire going for a brew,' said the boss. 'The Cup is on in 20 minutes', he added, producing a battered looking transistor radio.

I soon had a fire going, and the billy boiling, but I was still quite mystified. What was this Cup business? 'It'll be the Melbourne Cup for sure,' said Bob.

'But that's a fucking horse race more than 4,000 kilometres away,' I said in astonishment.

Turned out that my mate Bob was absolutely right. There in the vast Australian bush, miles from anywhere, four blokes supped billy tea and listened to about every third or fourth word of the 1968 Melbourne Cup broadcast. We heard enough to know that it was eventually won by a huge margin by a horse with the name of Rain Lover, with French sounding nag coming second.

'Did you back the winner?' I asked Mr Baines. 'Never backed a horse in my life,' came the reply. 'But never miss the Cup,' he added.

That night after dinner, my mate surprised me by bringing up some rather serious topics of conversation. We covered the assassinations of both Martin Luther King and Bobby Kennedy in the US earlier in the year, and the resulting protests in that country.

'That LBJ guy seems to be trying to make some progress inside the country,' Bob said with an impressive level of knowledge that I had yet to gain.

'But he's floundering with the Vietnam situation,' he continued. 'That Tet offensive caught the yanks napping last February and I reckon Johnson won't last long as President'.

It appeared that I had underestimated my travelling buddy.

Behind that comic mask was a very well-informed mind. Who would have guessed it?!

Towards the end of breakfast the next day, Mr Baines suddenly appeared.

'I have some paperwork and provision ordering today, so Brian has some work at the homestead for you two.'

After swallowing our final slices of toast and a second mug of tea, we followed Brian out to one of the large sheds.

'There's a swag of truck and car tyres with punctures here that you blokes are going to repair,' he said.

I looked at Bob, who simply shrugged his shoulders. We had no idea how to mend punctured tyres. I had only ever repaired bicycle tyres. Would it be the same?

Brian picked up a wheel and began looking for anything that may have penetrated the tyre wall or tread, eventually finding the head of a nail.

'Grab the pliers and pull that nail out, Bruce,' he said turning to grab another wheel. After much swearing and grunting, I eventually managed to pull it out.

Brian then grabbed a tyre lever and expertly removed the inner tube from the tyre.

'Let's pop some air into her, shall we?' he suggested, picking up an air hose that was connected to a compressor, blowing up the tube to about 30 PSI, and then taking the tube over to a large container of water.

'If we pop it into the water, we'll be able to see where the leak is', said Brian in a measured tone.

Shit, that's clever, I thought.

Brian then wiped the tube dry and marked the puncture location with a white marking pen. He produced a tyre repair kit that was indeed similar to a bicycle kit, meaning that I was now into half familiar territory.

With Brian watching on, I buffed up the rubber, surrounding

the leak with a wire brush. Brian showed me how to apply the sealant, check that it was airtight by again returning the tube to the water tub, pop the tube back into the tyre and fill it with air again from the compressor. Job done for tyre number one. Brian then left us to get on with the stack of tyres needing attention. Bob spent the rest of the morning cracking jokes about there being far too much hot air from me, his superior ability for inserting objects, and his intense pleasure in the art of buffing.

After enjoying the luxury of lunch in our dining room, Mrs Baines approached me.

'Now that you've finished with your tyre repairing, I've got a special job for you,' she said.

Brian and Bob made their exit quickly, leaving me to my fate. I followed the matron of the household as she led me out to the side of the main homestead to a large vegetable patch. Well, actually only about half the area was taken up with vegetables. The other half was filled with weeds.

'Once you remove all the weeds, kindly water the vegies with that watering can over there,' she said.

I spent the afternoon in solitude, completing the not unpleasant task. It made a welcome change to our usual arduous work out in the bush. At first, I simply enjoyed my own company for a change, but soon enough my thoughts drifted to worrying about Trish. I started fretting about how she was fairing without me, and if our relationship would stand the test of time.

That night I shared my back story with Bob for the first time. He listened quietly without interrupting, just periodically nodding his understanding. Finally, he looked me in the eye. I waited, half expecting him to turn the story into a humorous anecdote, but no, I had Bob in a serious mood again.

'That's a tough situation, for sure,' he said. 'But with the involvement of police enforcing the separation with your girl, you need to toughen up and continue your travelling until the year is up. If it's meant to be, you'll end up getting back together again. If not, you'll have to learn to live with it'.

It was simple and straightforward advice, admittedly given with a hard edge, but without doubt, delivered with complete honesty.

I digested his advice for a few moments.

'What about your background mate?' I asked switching the topic. 'And what was all that business with the coppers back in Perth that day?' I added.

'Let's just say that I've been a bit of a naughty boy at times, but I'd like to leave it at that Bruce.'

That was the end of my attempt to get to learn more about Bob's own back story.

He changed the subject by telling me a joke.

'What's red, and goes up and down?'

'I don't know Bob.

'A cherry in a lift.'

We were back to Bob the clown again.

12

KILLING TIME

As we were putting the dogs and everything else into the back of the ute after another hard day of herding sheep and marking lambs, Mr Baines turned to Brian.

'With these extra mouths to feed and the dogs eating a lot because of their workload, we're running low on meat again', he explained. 'So, could you organise the slaughtering of another sheep when we get back? And I reckon it's time one of these two learnt how to do the slaughtering,' pointing in our direction.

I sat beside Bob in the back of the ute, surrounded by the panting dogs, wondering which of the two of us was going to do the killing. It was one thing to watch someone else wielding a knife, but quite another to perform this function yourself. I felt decidedly uneasy. No sooner had we reached the homestead yard, when Brian looked over at me.

'Do you reckon you're up to the job Bruce?' he asked.

I nodded nervously. It was time to follow Bob's advice to toughen up.

We grabbed the nearest unsuspecting sheep from what I now knew to be the slaughter queuing yard. We forced it onto its side. Brian gave me the twine, and try as I might, I couldn't prevent my fingers from trembling a bit as I tied the poor animals' feet together. 'Do you want to use my knife or yours?' asked Brian.

'Mine,' I said simply.

'Is it bloody sharp?' persisted Brian.

'It is,' I answered coldly.

Bob and Brian picked up the baying sheep and placed it on its back on the wooden structure.

'Stick the knife in there,' commanded Brian, pointing to one side of the now shrieking animals' neck. 'Remember to quickly cut through to the base of the neck to sever the spine, before completing the cut.'

I tried to ignore the terrified eyes of my prey and concentrated on pushing the blade in. Fortunately, I found the spine immediately, cut through it, and finished severing the neck. The sheep's body convulsed a short time as the blood gushed out onto the ground. Once again, the dogs gleefully rushed in to slurp up the quickly congealing red fluid.

'Well done', shouted Brian. A perfect cut. You could easily get a job in an abattoir now.'

I smiled weakly.

'I guess I could do it whenever it becomes necessary,' I said. 'But I don't think that I could earn my living from the exercise.'

Bob slapped me heartily on the back, probably relieved that I had been set the task instead of him. I asked him why he wasn't joining in with the dogs' dining experience again tonight. He just laughed good naturedly.

As we sat enjoying a brew during a mid-afternoon smoko, Brian looked over to me and asked. 'Do you want to borrow my transistor again tonight, Bruce?'

'Yes please.'

We arrived back at the homestead to hear the hugely disappointing news that the mail had failed to arrive, which took the wind out of my good mood.

After the evening meal, I snuck off to bed with my highly treasured gift for the night. I lay in the dark listening intently as I twiddled with the dial. I eventually found Perth station 6KY again.

You bloody beauty – they were counting down the top ten songs of the week.

The reception was marginally better, so I was able to hear the presenter announce that the number 10 song was the Bee Gees 'I Just Gotta Get a Message to You'. I was greatly pleased with this news, as I was an ardent fan of this English/Aussie band. I hummed along. It had been in the charts for a good few months, so I knew it quite well from my time in Perth.

I frowned at the news that the 1910 Fruitgum Company were still charting so high with their abysmal '1-2-3 Red Light' piece of crap. My disgust deepened when I heard that Jeannie C Riley's 'Harper Valley PTA' was at number four. The reception continued to fade in and out, but I heard enough of a new Paul MacCartney song titled 'Those Were the Days' by Mary somebody, to approve heartily of the melody.

I waited with bated breath for the announcement of the number one song.

Yes, The Beatles were still at the top of the charts with their superb 'Hey Jude'. I lay there blissfully as that great song faded in and out for a sublime seven minutes.

I had just turned off the small receiving device when Bob returned to our sleeping quarters.

'Night Bob', I said snuggling down contentedly.

'Night mate,' came the reply as Bob settled down to sleep.

After about ten minutes Bob's voice rang out accusingly. 'You're not shaking ya bloody maracas are ya, Lowery?' he said.

'Nah, just reorganising the orchestra stalls mate,' I responded, giggling under my breath.

Mr Baines seemed to be softening. We finished our Saturday work just after we'd repaired some more fences and had some lunch. We headed back to the homestead for an afternoon of leisure. I must admit to some apprehension as we arrived. Would there be mail? Indeed, there was. There were letters from my Mum, Dad and from Pete, plus the huge bonus of my camera being returned by the bus company.

I was touched when Dad said that he kept a picture of me in his wallet, which he looked at often.

Mum's letter again produced a swarm of emotions within me:

> It's now about seven weeks to Xmas and the children are all talking about it. Geoff and Sue no longer believe in Santa, but John and Michael still do, thank goodness.
>
> I hope in time you'll forget Trish a bit. I'm not sure she was honest with you about what she did with that other boy, so it'll take a while for me to think kindly of her again. Quite frankly, I don't like to hear that she is seeing a psychologist. Now I have that off my chest, I won't ever mention it again. Promise.
>
> Look after yourself Bruce. We all hope you enjoy your travels. You'll have lots of ups and

downs I guess, but won't it all be something to tell your grandchildren about in years to come?

Pete's letter made me smile:

> Got your epistle last Friday week and it was great to hear from you. I didn't think you would write so soon, but I suppose you have a bit of spare time in the evenings - just like in O'Malley. Hope like Christ that you get your camera back. I think you had some tremendous shots, which would bring back some swinging memories in the years ahead.
>
> I'm labouring again in Vic Park. I clear about 60 plus bucks a week, which isn't bad.
>
> I bet it's getting bloody hot up there now. When we team up again, which I hope won't be long, I propose that we delay going further north, because of the heat. Let's continue our travels to some cooler parts. We can then hit the north sometime next year.

However, there was still nothing from Trish. I was crushed. I had not received any mail from her since leaving Perth, despite having written to her many times. What was going on?

The fact that Trish was seeing a psychologist worried me. Were her parents pressuring her into it? What the fuck were they doing to her? This was surely the reason why she hadn't written to me. She was being bloody brainwashed.

I wrote to Pete as a way of dealing with my swirling emotions.

> Just received your letter mate. It was good to hear from you again. Actually, I'm a bit blue at the moment and am thinking about returning to Perth soon (or maybe even home). Trish hasn't written to me since I arrived here, and in a letter from my mum today she told me that Trish is seeing a psychologist, so I'm a very confused guy now.
> Well, I'll go now, as I must pen another letter to Trish.
> See you soon.
> Your mate
> Bruce
> P.S. Growing my sidies longer

I was angry and brooding and slept badly as a result. I couldn't get the thought out my mind that Trish was being bullied into permanently ending our relationship. It was bad enough that we had been forced to separate for twelve months, but I worried that the situation was even worse than I realised.

'Better leave me be mate,' I said to Bob over breakfast. 'I wouldn't be very good company today'. It was Sunday so we had the day to ourselves.

He nodded his agreement. After we'd eaten, Brian popped his head around the corner. 'Not sure if we told you blokes, but the Baines and I are off to another station today for a barbeque and get together, so you're on your own until tomorrow.'

'How far away are the neighbours?' asked Bob.

'Oh, only about 80 or 90 miles I think,' replied Brian. 'Would you blokes like to do some shooting? I can lend you my rifle for the day'.

'Yep,' I said, knowing that it would take my mind off things.

Bob demurred, saying that he'd had enough of killing animals for a while.

'Well, if you're going hunting Bruce, please make sure you focus on feral animals,' said Brian. 'We're always happy to be culling those buggers.'

I spent the morning taking photos of Yaringa for the sake of posterity, but after lunch I took off on foot with a rifle, knife and a water bottle. I tried to clear my mind from the angry fog enveloping it. I needed a clear head to be out hunting in this vast region on my own, otherwise I could easily get lost. It also occurred to me that the largest animals I had shot previously were rabbits. I was after much bigger prey today.

I trudged off into the heat haze, encountering plenty of sheep and the occasional emu. Suddenly there were kangaroos everywhere, but I remembered the strong advice given to me by Brian and kept my powder dry. Those buggers moved too fast out here anyway. I wasn't that good a shot.

Eventually I encountered a trip of goats. Out front was a large male with a set of extremely large horns. He was followed closely by his harem of females and young kids, all trotting obediently behind King Billy. Here was my chance. I followed at a distance waiting to get a good bead on the trip leader. Eventually King Billy paused, sniffing the wind searching for signs of danger. By a stroke of luck (for me, anyway) I was about 25 yards away and downwind, but even so his instinct told him that something wasn't right. I tried to control my heavy breathing as I brought the rifle up to my shoulder, and looked down the barrel, fixing Billy in my sights.

I aimed at where I thought his heart would be and slowly squeezed the trigger. The shot rang out and Billy staggered to his knees, but almost as quickly regained his footing, taking off at pace with his brood in tow. Shit. He didn't go down for the count. I ran behind, chasing the trip, and only just keeping up.

Eventually I realised that Billy was slowing down. His cries of pain rent the air.

Bloody hell, I didn't expect hunting to cause this much extended suffering.

Suddenly Billy was on his knees with his trip gathered nearby. Everything started to slow down in my mind, as I ran up to him. The most merciful thing I could do now was to quickly finish him off with my knife, in the same way that I had dispatched the sheep a few days before.

Not so. There is world of difference to struggling with a large wounded wild male goat, who is fighting you to defend his harem, in comparison to slaughtering a largely docile sheep. Billy fought like hell, refusing to give me the opportunity to cleanly drive my knife into his throat. His eyes fixed on mine as he bleated out his defiance. I eventually grasped one of his horns and pulled his head back, driving the knife into his neck, searching for his spinal cord. His strength and ability to wriggle made this take longer than I wished, but eventually I felt the knife's blade cut through bone. Blood was spurting everywhere. Billy suddenly stopped struggling, and save for a few kicks, finally expired.

I sat down next to my vanquished prey. I felt sick. After a few minutes I realised there were a dozen sets of eyes looking at me. The nausea became more acute as I realised that Billy's family had just witnessed his killing at my hands.

'Toughen up,' I said to myself as I began to cut off Billy's horns.

But the nausea and feeling of guilt wouldn't go away. The

family of goats were still gathered at Billy's side when I left the scene with my prized horns. I vomited a couple times as I made my way back to the Yaringa homestead.

13

AN UNFAIR WHACK

Bob had been duly impressed by the size of my hunting trophies when I had returned the night before. He continued to express his amazement over breakfast.

'Shit, judging by the size of those horns, that fucking goat must have been huge. How did you manage that?' he asked me, wanting to know all the details.

I still wasn't proud of myself, so I made light of my so-called hunting prowess. Apart from that I was still worried about what was happening to Trish back home. I had again stewed with my thoughts throughout another fairly sleepless night alternating in my half sleep between visions of Trish in distress and the recollection of King Billy looking me in the eye defiantly as I struggled to overcome him.

I'd woken up with a resolution. I'd pass in my notice, make my way back to Perth so I could return to Melbourne more easily if Trish needed me. I confided this to Bob, who simply shrugged his shoulders, saying, 'Your call mate.'

Brian came in to see us after breakfast.

'How was your day yesterday?' he asked.

'Well, all I did was to sit on my arse all day,' boomed Bob. 'But the great white hunter here scooped the pool.'

Brian looked over at me quizzically, but Bob didn't give me time to answer. He quickly picked up King Billy's great horns, showing them to an impressed Brian.

'Look what our raggedy arsed mate bagged,' said Bob.

'Great work Bruce. Knocking out the leader of the pack is always the most effective way to cull,' enthused Brian. 'And goats are among the worst of the feral animals up here.' I felt marginally better after hearing his rationale.

'We're off in a northerly direction this morning,' said Brian. There are quite a few sheep in that corner of the property that we haven't seen for quite a while, so we're in for a busy day herding and marking again.' 'Fine with me,' I said. 'But I'd like a word with Mr Baines before we go'.

'Okay' replied Brian. 'He's in the office, so follow me'.

I knocked on the door of the office and Mr Baines looked up from reading some paperwork.

'Well, what do you want?' he said, obviously annoyed at the interruption.

'Due to some personal matters, I'm afraid I have to pass in a week's notice,' I informed the boss.

'What the hell?' he spluttered. 'You've only just got here'.

'Sorry sir, but I have no choice.'

He just sat there, staring at me. After what seemed to be an eternity, he spoke. 'I'll have your money made up next Saturday morning. You can leave straight after breakfast. Now get out of my sight.'

'How'd Baines take the news?' asked Bob as we prepared for the day's labours.

'Not very well mate,' I replied. 'I'll be leaving next Saturday morning, and I reckon this week will be hell'.

My prediction was spot on. The boss waved a big stick for us all that day but singled me out repeatedly for the dirtiest of tasks and the heaviest criticism.

That night, Bob kept up a barrage of hilarious jokes. Eventually, even he had to pause to catch his breath. We were wheezing with laughter. I knew the jokes were just a feint to cover his feelings. I reached out and grabbed his arm.

'I'm sorry to be leaving so abruptly mate.'

'Not a problem at all. It's just part of life, and ya gotta do what ya gotta do.'

'But...'

'Look Bruce, I'm going to be fine here. Don't worry about a thing.'

There was no point in pursuing the matter further. The humour returned for the remainder of the evening, but it did seem a little forced.

After breakfast, we travelled in the ute for ages. The dogs were blissfully ignorant of my black mood and were bouncing from one side of the tray to the other in an effort to see what was happening in the harsh landscape. They would occasionally slurp our faces with their wet tongues. Their activities lightened my heart. It was a joy to see them so happy.

'Shit – we're really going walkabout today,' yelled Bob, leaning over the side of the ute to use his bushman's handkerchief.

'Yep,' I agreed. 'I reckon Baines is heading off to find the oldest lambs on Yaringa, just so you and I get a good workout today.'

'Ah, that's no wucka's for us,' shrugged my big mate. 'You and I can handle anything these buggers can throw at us.'

By afternoon smoko, Bob nearly had to eat his words. The boss had taken us to the furthest reaches of the outback known to any white fella. We had run the longest distances yet, chasing the dumbest and most timid sheep in creation, eventually herding them into another crude set of pens. The heat was so intense and debilitating that the cool water from the canvas bags failed to quench our raging thirst, no matter how much of it we drank. Once we had jumped into the smallest pen, we quickly realised that my prediction about lifting the heaviest lambs to date, had become a reality.

As we sat around the afternoon fire, gratefully raising brews of hot black tea to our lips, Bob looked over at me, his face splattered with dried sheep's blood.

'I knew we hadn't come here to fuck spiders,' Bob said quietly. 'But today's almost been enough to make a bloke cark it.'

'Sorry mate,' I whispered back. 'I think the boss is trying to make me suffer, and I'm afraid you're getting caught in the crossfire.'

'S'awright mate,' replied Bob with a wink. 'I guess it's not your fault that you're a boofhead'.

The bottle of beer with dinner that night had never tasted better.

AFTER A MORNING of more fence repairing, and as we were sitting around the midday campfire with the usual mutton sandwiches and mugs of tea, Mr Baines looked over at Bob.

'I've got a replacement worker coming Friday to help you,' he said, ignoring my presence completely. 'His name is Ralph and I expect you to help get him settled in quickly.'

Bob just nodded, and Brian said nothing.

To be honest, I was surprised that Bob was staying on. The pay was lousy, considering how hard we worked.

Brian appeared as we were finishing our breakfast.

'New job for you today fellas,' he announced. Have either of you done any house painting before?'

'Only a bit,' I replied, but Bob assured him he had done quite a lot.

Brian took us around to the back of the homestead where it was shaded from the sun. 'This whole back wall of the house needs to be sanded back, cleaned down with sugar soap, and then painted with an undercoat, before finishing off with a final coat.'

We made our way to a large, locked shed where Brian furnished us with a couple of double-sided ladders, a solid plank to place in between them, plus some large brushes, cleaning materials and tins of paint.

We returned to the side of the homestead that needed our complete attention for the day.

'It was good of Brian to have us work in the shade,' I said.

'He had no bloody alternative numb nuts,' replied Bob. 'This here is oil-based paint, and ya can't brush it on in direct sunlight'.

'And I thought he was being kind.'

We were out of sight from everyone as we toiled with sandpaper, rags, brushes and brooms, and finally cleaning the vast wall with sugar soap. It took us until late morning to complete the cleaning process because Bob also had to plug some small holes and sand some additional spots on the windowsills. He really did have experience with this painting lark.

After lunch, we returned to the task in hand. As we began to paint the wall with the undercoat, I decided to fuck around a bit, and started my own version of applying some temporary graffiti.

BAINESVILLE, I wrote in large letters. A WEST AUSTRALIAN PARADISE.

The paint was dripping with sarcasm. Suddenly Bob looked over at me and said quietly, 'Bandits at 3 o'clock.'

I spun round to see Mr Baines approaching from the far end of the driveway. I plunged my brush into the tin and quickly spread paint over the offending words. Bob, God bless his cotton socks, assisted with the cover up. The boss strode over.

'Smartarse,' was all he said before walking briskly past us.

His use of the word 'smartarse' in the singular, indicated that he had no doubts as to who the real culprit was.

THE NEXT DAY, Bob and I were again sent off to the rear of the homestead, complete with ladders, brushes and paint. We worked through the day wielding the brushes, and chatting about everything and anything, just as long as Bob could find some humour in it. 'S'pose you'll go back to Jonkers and find a job shovelling shit again?' he said.

'Yeah, I guess so,' I replied. 'In his last letter to me Pete told me he was clearing $60 for a six-day week in Perth, working in the building trade as a labourer. That's a fuck sight more than we're getting up here.'

'They'll be working his arse off for that though,' said Bob.

'Yep, not like the cushy lifestyle here at Yaringa,' I laughed. 'You should still consider coming back to Perth too'.

Bob stopped his painting and looked at me seriously. 'Remember those cops that pulled us over that day in Perth?' said Bob. 'Well, those guys are still looking for me, and they won't give up easily. Once they have enough evidence, they'll nail me for sure. I'm staying here, out of harm's way'.

Midway through the afternoon, I spotted a lone figure opening the station gate and slowly make his way towards the homestead.

'No doubt that'll be the new bloke Ralph,' I said. 'Let's go and greet him'.

'Yeah, 'agreed Bob. 'I guess we can try to cushion the blow a bit'.

We walked over to him.

'G'day,' I said to the newcomer.

He was thin, bespectacled and rather short.

'You're Ralph I s'pose?'

He nodded his acknowledgment, squinting at us through the heat.

'I'm Bob and this here is Bruce,' said my mate. 'But don't take him too seriously, he's leaving tomorrow cause he's a bit weak ya see.'

Ralph seemed to take all this quite seriously, confining his question to Bob. 'Who should I report to, and where?'

'Make sure you go around to the back door,' replied Bob. 'Ask for Mr Baines, prepare to grovel a lot in his presence, and you'll get on fine,' he finished.

Ralph took all this in and headed off in the direction that Bob had shown him. 'I would've warned him about you, but he wouldn't have believed that you were that big a prick,' I grinned at Bob.

'He'll learn soon enough,' replied Bob, still staring at the back of the newcomer as he trudged towards the homestead.

That night at dinner, Ralph held on to every word that Bob uttered throughout the meal, whilst ignoring me. Either he had taken Bob's initial comments as gospel, or the boss had put in a bad word about me. It didn't matter much to me. I'd be gone tomorrow. But it was a shame how much bullshit Bob was filling Ralphs brain with.

Bob spoke convincingly about giant goannas that ate sheep and kangaroos that were so big and ferocious that they could stand on their tail, pick a bloke up with their forearms, and rip you down the middle with their hind legs. Ralph went pale. I hoped he would latch on to Bob's humour sooner rather than later. That night, as I drifted off to sleep, I could vaguely make out Bob's chilling description of a 10-metre snake that had been known to swallow camels with ease.

. . .

THE CONVERSATION over breakfast between Bob, Ralph and myself was proving to be rather stilted. Either Bob had run out of hair-raising stories for Ralphs educational benefit, or the latter had finally twigged to the bullshit.

For my part, I was acutely aware that I was leaving within the next hour or so, and that the strong friendship between Bob and I was going to be severed. I was about to try again to articulate my feelings when we were interrupted by Brian's entry to the room.

'Mr Baines would like to see you in the office now Bruce,' he said in a voice that sounded a bit strained.

'Okay,' I said, putting down a half-eaten slice of toast.

'I've got to get the dogs in the truck now, so I'll say goodbye and thanks', Brian said warmly shaking my hand. 'The bus should be passing between 11 and 11.30.'

I knocked on the office door. Mr Baines looked up and strode quickly to the doorway, thrusting an envelope into my hand.

'Here's your final pay packet,' he said brusquely.

'Thank you.'

I was going to add my goodbyes but was thwarted from doing so by the boss turning on his heel, and walking to his desk, where he kept his back to me. Sensing bad news, I stayed standing at the office door and opened the envelope.

The total amount of money inside came the grand total of $1.25.

'Excuse me Mr Baines,' I said, still keeping my tone respectful. 'There appears to be a mistake here. I thought I was being paid $19 a week'.

The boss turned around sharply. 'You should read your contract again,' he spat. 'It's $19 a *fortnight* including board and lodging, but less expenses. I pulled the handwritten explanatory note from my pay packet. It read that my total pay for four weeks work after tax was $38 with expenses listed at $36.25 and deducted.

'May I ask what these expenses are for?', I asked, finally coming to the realisation that I was experiencing foul play.

'Tobacco and beer,' came the abrupt reply.

I began to calculate the money involved.

'At no point in offering us a bottle of beer each night did you mention that you were going to charge us for it,' I said evenly. 'And even when you take into account the two tins of out-of-date Log Cabin tobacco you gave me, that makes the price of each bottle of beer around a $1.20, which is more than double the going rate,' I reasoned. 'Everything has to be freighted here, and that costs a lot of money,' came the boss's firm reply.

I stood silently for a few seconds, before calmly delivering my final words to Mr Baines. 'Since arriving here I have always thought you to be a hard, but fair man,' I said, trying to keep my voice low and even. 'But I now know I was wrong about your fairness,' I finished.

'Leave the premises immediately,' came the abrupt reply, as the boss closed the office door in my face.

I hurried back to our sleeping quarters to find Bob. He was about to leave the room when I bailed him up, angrily explaining the rort in my pay.

'If you're staying on, you had better sort this out for yourself mate,' I said.

Bob looked me in the eye.

'I can take care of this for myself Bruce,' he said quietly. 'But right now, I just need to shake your hand.'

I took his great beefy mitt firmly in mine, maintaining our eye contact for some time before he eventually winked and grinned broadly.

'Hooroo,' was the only other word Bob uttered, as he turned and strode out the door.

I watched from the doorway as he walked quickly to the waiting truck without turning around. He jumped in the back with the eternally joyful dogs, and his new chum. He waved briefly in my general direction as the truck took off, quickly gathering speed in a whirl of dust.

I slowly packed up my things, including the two goat horns. Apart from a few photographs, and some interesting memories, the horns would be the only objects that I would be taking away from Yaringa.

I made it down to the main road by 10.30 and found some shade under a sparse bush to sit down to wait for the bus. I had considered saying farewell and thanks to Mrs Baines before leaving the homestead but decided against it. Discretion was the better part of valour, so I had simply walked away.

I looked through my papers, quickly finding my employment contract with Sheffield Employment. Sure enough, it stated that my pay at Yaringa was to be $19 clear, including full board and keep.

What it failed to record was whether this was weekly, fortnightly, or even bloody monthly, which gave the management plenty of flexibility of course.

'Bastards,' I swore.

I checked my wallet.

Thank God I had miraculously found those few bank notes, lying in the wilderness on my day of arrival. If not for that amazing stroke of luck, I would be almost penniless and stranded almost 500 miles from Perth.

As it was, I just had enough to pay for the bus fare with a few dollars to spare.

I sat on the side of the road still fuming to myself, eventually convincing myself that I had earned myself some fun on a

Saturday night. Fuck it! I made the rash decision to stop the night in Geraldton. If I ran low on dough, I could always hitch hike back to Perth. I'd done that before, hadn't I?

The bus eventually appeared in the distance, slowing to a halt in the heat haze.

'A ticket to Geraldton please,' I said brightly.

'That'll be 10 bucks 'mate,' replied the driver.

I sat at the back of the near empty bus, settling in for the four-hour journey.

14

BACK DOWN SOUTH

The bus rumbled into the fair town of Geraldton in the late afternoon. As I was getting off, I asked the bus driver for his recommendation for cheap accommodation.

'I think the Geraldton Hotel in Gregory Street is pretty good,' he offered.

After asking a few locals about how to get there, I found myself in front of an old pub. It looked pretty good to me. I made my way through the front doors to reception.

'How much for a single room for the night?' I asked the receptionist.

'All the rooms at the front are $10 a night, which includes breakfast in the dining room,' she answered. Perhaps noticing my bedraggled appearance, she added, 'But we also have budget rooms out the back for $8, and that still includes breakfast.'

'Thanks, I'll take one of those,' I said proffering her a sunburnt $10 note.

The room seemed pretty darn luxurious. It was quite stylish and clean, with crisp white sheets on the bed. I checked and counted my remaining currency. It totalled $8.25. That would do for a slap-up meal and a few beers. I'd have to hitchhike tomorrow. I was again sticking to my usual philosophy of live for the moment. In my present predicament it didn't pay to think too far ahead.

'Any live music in town tonight?', I asked the kindly receptionist on my way out of the hotel.

'Yes, I think one of our local bands The Undecided will be playing at The Freemasons Hotel tonight, and we reckon they're pretty damn good,' she added with a fair amount of enthusiasm.

'Sounds good to me,' I replied.

Live music was in reach at last. I spent the next two hours wandering around the town. Perched right beside the sea it was most picturesque. Clean and tidy, it had the appearance of being relatively prosperous. After all the constant hard work in the roughest of Australian bush settings over the past month, this town seemed like manna from heaven.

After a long and lingering shower, I put on a clean shirt that matched my tight fitting Leisuremaster pin stripe stretch blue slacks. I then made my way to the Freemasons Hotel where I sat perched on a bar stool in the front bar ordering a mixed grill and a cold beer. Fortunately, the meal that arrived was huge. I hadn't eaten since breakfast, so I tucked in with relish. I could hear a band warming up from somewhere at the back of the pub. They certainly did sound good.

Finishing my meal, I made my way towards the sound of music. I entered a sizeable room that was already full of young guys and chicks as the music started up nice and loud. The Undecided was a mod band consisting of five members. They were performing an alright cover version of the Kinks 'You Really Got Me'. The dance area had filled up quickly and I had no trouble finding numerous friendly female dance partners immediately.

After a while I took a break and stood watching the action

and listening to the band. They had now warmed up properly and were getting better as the night moved on. Suddenly a bloke about my own age gave me a nudge.

'Fancy another beer?' he shouted at me.

'I'm afraid I'm skint, so I can't get into a shout, but thanks anyway,' I yelled back.

He nodded, headed off to the bar and came back with two large 16oz glasses of chilled beer.

'Ya don't have to worry about shouting me back. I know what it's like to be broke.'

'Thanks and cheers,' I beamed back at my new acquaintance, turning my attention back towards the sweating and heaving female dancers, as they moved to the rhythmic beat. 'Gary's the name,' persisted my beer supplier.

'Bruce,' I bellowed back, taking a good swig of the amber fluid.

The band eventually took a break saying they would be back in 10 minutes for the final session of the night.

'What do ya think of the band?' asked Gary.

'They're very young, but I reckon they could go places,' I replied. 'Their covers of The Kinks and The Troggs in particular are pretty much spot on.'

'Yeah, and they're local lads too,' enthused Gary, who was proving to be quite knowledgeable about rock music in general. 'Another beer?' he asked.

'Only if you're sure,' I said in return. Gary soon came back with another two 16oz glasses of the brown stuff, one of which I wolfed down quickly, not wishing to miss dancing the last session.

Both Gary and I found two willing and attractive chicks to groove with. The last set included 'Wild Thing' and 'All of the Day and All of the Night', both of which had the jam-packed dancers stomping with even greater energy. Eventually the

Undecided finally made a decision and finished off their set with 'I Can't Control Myself', to much acclaim. Unfortunately, both the chicks we had been dancing with clearly had no problem in controlling themselves. They thanked us politely and made for the exit.

I looked over at Gary, who smiled back.

'Would you like to come back to my place to listen to some music and have a few more beers?' he asked.

'What, just the two of us?' I asked.

Gary's face flushed red. 'Only if you'd like to,' he stammered.

I twigged.

'Oh Gary,' I said looking him straight in the eye, are you putting the hard word on me?' He paused looking down at his shoes. It was the first time this had ever happened to me, and despite formerly thinking that I would belt any gay guy who tried it on with me, I actually felt strangely flattered, and sorry for Gary at the same time.

'Sorry mate, but my sexual interests lie squarely with the opposite sex.'

'I'm sorry Bruce,' said Gary despondently. 'I guess I picked you wrong.'

'Sure did,' I replied. 'Please don't tell anybody though,' pleaded Gary. 'Nobody in this town knows that I'm gay'.

'Your secret's safe with me,' I reassured him. 'Any chance of a final beer?'

As I sat alone on my comfortable bed in my hotel room, I pondered what had just happened. Strangely, I still didn't feel cheapened or threatened by Gary's approach. I had already known that I had zero interest in a homosexual encounter, but my anticipation of some kind of violent reaction from myself hadn't been realised.

Instead, I now had some understanding of the excruciating pain and loneliness that a gay guy like Gary experienced on a daily basis in an Australian country town like Geraldton. My final thought before drifting off to sleep in my luxurious bed was to wonder whether I should consider ditching my tight-fitting blue pin stripe Leisuremaster slacks.

What a bloody amazing day.

I AROSE the next morning after enjoying a deep sleep in my luxurious surroundings, which baffled me momentarily as I awoke. But slowly the bits and pieces of the events of the previous day fell into place.

Breakfast was high on the agenda, but what was I going to do after that, given that I had no more than a few coins left in my pocket? I roused myself and again stayed in the shower a bit longer than I should. Fresh, clean, non-bore water sprayed over my body, and the hotel soap felt infinitely superior in softness to the Sunlight Soap I had been using at Yaringa. Pure luxury.

I finally made my way downstairs, but suddenly paused in the corridor to listen to the music being piped through the hotel sound system. Yes, it was that McCartney song that I had first heard fading in and out on the transistor radio a few weeks before at Yaringa, performed by some dame. I listened intently.

The announcer advised that the song was performed by Mary Hopkin, but that it was in fact written many years before in Russia. McCartney had instead produced the recording but hadn't written it. Regardless it was something very special to me at that moment. Apparently, it was number two on the Australian charts that week, only being kept out of the top spot by the Beatles 'Hey Jude', which had been in that position for weeks on end.

The dining room was only half full as I selected a table in the corner and began choosing some breakfast tucker from the buffet. When I sat back down with my plate full of food and a steaming mug of tea, I noticed that the adjacent table was occupied by two attractive birds about the same age as myself, together with a guy who looked to be in his mid-twenties.

One of the chicks looked over in my direction and smiled. 'Come on over and join us,' she beckoned. 'No good sitting all by yourself'.

'Thank you,' I replied without hesitation, moving over to their table with my food and drink in tow.

'Maureen's my name, and my friend here is Vicki,' said my latest female acquaintance. 'And this here is Phil, who kindly offered us a ride from Carnarvon to Perth.'

The girls shook hands with me warmly, but it seemed to me that Phil was a little less enthusiastic.

'Vicki and I have been working in Carnarvon for a couple of months, but we're heading home now to Albany.'

'What have you been up to?'

I explained my time at Yaringa Station, which seemed to interest both girls a good deal. 'Yeah, but I'm hitch hiking back to Perth now, and probably back to Melbourne after that,' I said, trying a little too hard to appear heroic. 'And what will you do there?' asked Vicki.

'Oh, probably get a rock band together,' I replied vaguely.

At that time, I could barely strum a guitar, but thought that my reply would probably impress my new audience even further.

'Ooh,' smiled Maureen. 'So, we might be sitting next to a future rock star then.'

'Who knows?' I replied, smiling.

Suddenly Vicki turned to Phil, who appeared to have only been half interested in the conversation, preferring to concentrate on his corn flakes.

'We have room in the car for Bruce don't we Phil?'

The designated driver stirred himself, looked over at me, and replied, 'Maybe Bruce already has a lift?'

He was clearly reluctant to share the company of two attractive females for the four hour journey south. At least not with a tanned and blond would-be young rock star, who was clearly full of himself, and whom he had only just met.

Fearing a lost opportunity, I quickly confirmed that he would be doing me a great service by offering me a lift. The two birds stared at Phil, waiting for his answer.

'Well okay, I suppose we can help him out,' said Phil slowly and hesitantly.

'Excellent. I'm sure we'll have some fun along the way,' Maureen said, finalising my travel arrangements in an instant. Lady luck appeared to be shining on me at last.

The sun was indeed shining as the four us made our way to the hotel car park. Phil strode purposely towards a shiny near new GT Falcon, unlocked it, and opened the boot.

'You beauty,' I thought as I gleefully threw my swag inside. We're riding in style.

The ride down to Lancelin was indeed great fun as the chicks and I talked almost nonstop about our musical interests, clothing fashions, the accuracy of horoscopes, as well as many other wonderfully superficial, yet amusing topics. Phil barely uttered a word as the powerful vehicle sped us smoothly and quickly southwards. We eventually pulled into the scenic seaside town for a comfort stop at the public toilets.

'How about a takeaway coffee?' suggested Phil after we had left the toilet block and were walking off towards a promising looking café.

With a fair degree of embarrassment, I explained my financial predicament, and inability to shout. The girls happily said that was no problem, and that they would be pleased to pay. Phil screwed up his nose in disgust.

'Come and give me a hand Bruce,' said Maureen brightly.

As we were waiting for the coffees to be made, she looked up at me.

'Vicki and I are so pleased that you're travelling with us,' she explained. We're sure that Phil thought we would be so taken with his big donk of a car, that we would be easy targets for him, but a fancy car doesn't guarantee sex appeal in a bloke. You being with us has helped to straighten things out.'

About half an hour down the road, Phil slowed the car down and pulled over into the gravel. Both the girls looked over at me with apprehension. They needn't have worried. The car's rear driver's side wheel had a tyre as flat as a pancake.

'Shit,' said Phil in a rather panicky voice. 'I have absolutely no idea how to fix that,' he added dejectedly.

'Not a problem,' I said bristling with authority. 'I'll have it replaced in no time.'

My training at Yaringa was standing me in good stead already.

For the remainder of the journey down to Perth, Phil's attitude towards me changed completely. He became much more animated and readily joined in the bright conversation, even cracking some quite good jokes. It appeared that making myself useful had totally altered his perspective of me. As we entered the suburbs of Perth, I directed Phil to my previous place of abode in Mount Lawley.

As soon as we pulled up, the girls jumped out of the car and embraced me, planting moist kisses on my cheek. Phil pumped my hand vigorously. It's amazing how quickly you can sometimes make such warm friendships in such a short period of time. I waved at the disappearing GT Falcon as it took off at speed. I then turned towards the front door of Jonkers' Boarding House.

I found my good mate Pete in the largest of the shared

bedrooms, writing letters, obviously in deep concentration, and oblivious to everything going on around him. 'How are ya mate?' I said breezily, flopping down on the nearest bed. 'Bet ya didn't expect to see me this soon.'

'Bruce,' responded Pete beaming at me with a broad smile and thrusting his hand into mine. 'It's bloody great to see you.'

Our ability to confide with each other without embarrassment since leaving home made it relatively easy for me to not only explain my circumstances fully to my mate, but to also ask if he could loan me some money until I got myself back on my feet again. Once again, the response from my mate was immediate and positive.

'Sure buddy, I've put some money aside, so I can lend you a week's rent here plus another ten bucks to tide you over,' said Pete without hesitation. 'And I reckon there may be a chance that I could get you a job where I work on a building site,' he added confidently.

Jesus, had my luck changed or what?

Ma Jonkers did indeed have a bed available for me, so I joined the other inmates at the dinner table that evening. As we sat down, Pete introduced me to a smiling guy with black wavy hair, and a short goatee beard.

'This here is Barry Brogan, who also works with me at the building site,' said Pete. 'Apart from being a bloody Kiwi, he's quite a decent bloke,' continued Pete. 'He's just come back from travelling overseas, so I've been picking his brains about the best countries to visit'.

'G'day Barry,' I said warmly shaking his hand. 'Where did you travel to?'

'Quite a few countries, but two of the best were England and Sweden,' replied Barry without hesitation.

I quickly warmed to my new acquaintance as he recalled the highlights of swinging London, from seeing bands like The

Kinks, Spencer Davis Group and Cream live to the wide availability of groovy clothing styles on Carnaby Street, not yet seen in Australia. His tales had an understated plausibility about them, which impressed me. My inbuilt bullshit detector was beginning to become quite refined, and this guy was refreshingly honest about his exploits, which, in a strange way were made all the more intriguing by the total absence of unnecessary exaggeration.

'I'll keep my stories about Sweden and Swedish birds for another time,' Barry grinned, as we finished our meal. I was going to like this guy!

'So, tell us a bit about what you did up North Bruce,' said Peter, suddenly remembering that I must have had some interesting yarns to tell from my travels too.

'Well, I got my camera back from the bus company, and took some pretty interesting photos, so I'll show you more about Yaringa when I have the film processed,'

'But what was Geraldton like?' persisted Pete. I thought for a moment.

'Not bad, but I knocked back a root there,' I said with a careless shrug.

'You what?' exclaimed Pete. 'You've never knocked back sex in your life.' 'Nah, he just wasn't my type,' I replied with a grin.

I hit the hay early after hearing that we'd be picked at 7am the next morning to head off to work. Breakfast would be at 6.30. Boy, was I tired.

15

HARD YAKKA AGAIN

I was woken from my deep slumber by Pete shaking my shoulder and saying, 'Come on sleeping beauty; breakfast is in five minutes.'

I wandered into the already crowded bathroom, and elbowed my way to a sink, splashing cold water over my face, and blinking my eyes rapidly, in order to shake off my drowsiness. I'd only just managed to swallow some toast and tea, when Pete jumped up from the breakfast table. 'Time to go boys,' he said. 'Our lift doesn't wait if we're not ready on time.'

'What about our lunches?' I asked, thinking about my stomach as usual. 'Things have changed,' Pete yelled back. The Jonkers don't supply lunches as part of our board anymore, so we have to buy something'.

Pete, Barry and I jumped into an ageing Holden sedan.

'Who's the new bloke?' the driver asked.

'Nobby, meet Bruce,' announced Pete.' I'm gonna try and get him a job onsite.'

Nobby nodded his sunburnt face. 'Maybe the boss will take the opportunity to get rid of that lazy prick Wally,' he said approvingly, before turning up the car radio to a truly ear-splitting volume level.

We finally pulled up at the building site. 'We're building a whole block of apartments, so there's plenty of work for weeks to come,' explained Barry, as Pete made a beeline for the site foreman. The grizzled, wiry and serious looking boss exchanged some brief words with Pete, who turned around beckoning me to join them. 'Bruce, meet Kevin. He hires and fires around here,' said Pete. 'I've told him that you're a hard worker looking for a break'.

Kevin looked me up and down making an on the spot assessment. 'Where've you been working before this?' he asked me directly.

'I've just come back from working on a sheep station up north,' I replied.

'Hard Yakka up there?' queried Kevin, watching me closely for my response. 'Yes,' I replied. 'But I've never complained about hard work, if the pay is fair.' 'Yep, I've heard that some stations up north underpay their staff,' said Kevin. 'Is that why you left?'

'In part,' I confided.

'Wait here,' commanded Kevin, as he strode off towards the other end of the building site. Pete and Barry moved off towards a large stack of bricks, leaving me to wait on my own for the outcome of the boss's deliberations. I kept my fingers crossed. I needed this job badly.

I could see the foreman talking to some bloke in the distance, who seemed to be arguing back. Finally, Kevin straightened himself up and appeared to bring the discussion to an end by strenuously pointing his finger straight at the gate. The bloke stalked off, yelling something indecipherable, yet obviously venomous, over his shoulder in the general direction of the foreman.

Kevin made his way straight back to me. 'We'll give you a try out today son,' he said simply enough.

'If you're good enough, the job is six days a week at the same pay as your buddies,' he added. 'Work hard, be honest, use your initiative, and we'll get on fine. For the time being, your job, together with the other labourers, is to get bricks and mortar up to bricklayers, and they don't take kindly to running out of either.'

'Thanks Boss, you won't regret this,' I replied, jogging off to join my mates.

'I've got a full day to prove myself,' I said enthusiastically to Pete and Barry.

'Great stuff,' they both said in unison.

'Barry is mixing the mud, so you take it to the brickies using that barrow and spade,' advised Pete.' I'll be carting bricks with these other guys,' he finished, pointing in the direction of two other fit looking young blokes.

The morning passed quickly enough as Barry filled up my barrow with a mixture of cement, sand and water from his rotating mixer every time I returned from spading out the mud from the barrow to each of the brick layers, who were spread out throughout the site. I reached them along a network of strong wooden boards that had been carefully laid out for that purpose.

The fitness I had gained from chasing sheep through the bush stood me in good stead, as each brickie worked at a furious pace, making it necessary for me to continually run with my barrow in order to keep up with their demands. I couldn't help but notice that Pete and his brick-supplying mates, were also working at a similar pace, as each of us timed our runs to avoid, what would undoubtedly be a painful collision, if we didn't. It was hard work in the hot sun, but working as a team, made it worthwhile.

During the morning smoko, I saw Pete approach each tradesman and labourer on site, making copious notes on a tiny note pad and taking small sums of money from them. Eventually he reached me. 'What do ya want for lunch?' he asked.

'A couple of meat pies and a vanilla slice would be good,' I responded, passing him the $10 note he had lent me the night before. He then disappeared off site for about 10 minutes.

Just before the lunch break, Pete wandered off site again, returning right on midday carrying a large cardboard box, and immediately started passing out all the lunch orders to the waiting ravenously hungry workers. 'Do you do that every day?' I asked my mate.

'No, that role is divided up amongst all of the labourers, so we all get a shot at it,' Pete explained. 'It's an opportunity to get a break from the hard graft, and if it's handled carefully, can be quite profitable.'

'How come it's profitable?' I asked.

'Well, it's a time-honoured tradition that, providing the lunch organiser isn't greedy, it's acceptable for some small rounding off to happen when calculating the change on each order,' he continued with a noticeable degree of relish in his voice. 'I've made 35 cents today.'

'Oh,' I said, making a mental note about this lucrative, yet apparently acceptable daily scam. 'Can I get the lunches tomorrow?'

'You can wait your bloody turn,' came the immediate reply.

At the end of the day foreman Kevin approached me, and without any facial expression whatsoever, stated with masterful brevity, 'You can turn up again tomorrow son.' Yippee!

THE NEXT WORKING day commenced with Pete taking over the job of delivering mud to the waiting brickies, while I was redirected to carting bricks. Remembering the advice I had received previously about the wear and tear on hands when handling bricks all day, I looked in vain for some gloves or slabs of rubber. When I couldn't find anything suitable, I just got stuck in, not wishing to appear soft.

Later as I was enjoying my lunch of two salad rolls and washing them down with a large bottle of bitter lemon for additional energy, the conversation took a serious turn. It was led by a guy by the name of Ralph who made his anti-Vietnam War sentiments well known.

'The new US President Nixon has got himself elected on the basis that he will end that bloody war soon,' he said forcefully. 'We'll see if he's fair dinkum or not, in time.' I kept my lip buttoned, but listened carefully as Ralph heatedly extolled the evil that we, and our American allies, were allegedly perpetrating in South East Asia.

'We've already had over 150 Aussie diggers die in that damn country,' Ralph continued with pure venom in his voice. I didn't know that, and actually felt a bit guilty for being so ignorant.

Before this, I had simply listened to the official government line that we were involved to prevent the spread of dreaded communism, just like we did in Korea, but here was guy putting forward an entirely different point of view. Knowing my brother Bob could soon be serving with the Australian Army in that conflict made me feel distinctly uncomfortable. 'Did you know that over 1,000 antiwar protesters marched to Pentridge Prison a week or so, back in Melbourne, in support of jailed conscientious objector John Zarb,' asserted Ralph.

'The antiwar movement is gaining momentum and we'll stop it for sure,' he concluded.

'Well, there'll be no protesting on this work site,' said our foreman Kevin quietly, in a way that made it clear that the conversation should end. Nevertheless, we all recommenced work that afternoon thinking a bit differently about the war. Surely our government knew what they were doing. Didn't they?

When we arrived back at the boarding house, I found it almost impossible to open the door, there was so little skin left on the tips of my fingers. It even proved a difficult task to write some letters home to the family and Trish, but I had to let them know that I'd left Yaringa and was now back in Perth. I begged Trish to write soon. Not hearing from her was starting to tear me apart.

KEVIN GAVE me two slabs of thick rubber as I arrived on site the next morning with just a glint of a grin on his face.

'These should help a bit son,' he said quietly.

I thanked him profusely and managed to get through the day without losing too much more skin from my fingers. We were all stripped naked to the waist in the West Australian sun, becoming as brown as berries in the process.

'Once your skin thickens up, ya don't burn anymore,' we preached to each other, giving clear precedent to looking fashionably tanned in our constant endeavour to attract the opposite sex. We'd heard rumours about skin damage from too much sun exposure but thought this was a bit exaggerated.

That evening after dinner Barry started reminiscing about his recent travels overseas. 'Tell us a bit about the groups you saw live in England again,' I urged. 'Which ones did you like the best?'

'I reckon The Spencer Davis Group were the best blues band in the UK with that young Stevie Winwood capturing the essence of the blues better than anybody else, but unfortunately Stevie left the band early last year. Their hit singles 'Keep on

Running' and 'Gimme Some Lovin' are great, but when they performed live, it was another level again. My outright favourite live band is The Kinks. They've progressed from the early hard rocking numbers like 'You Really Got Me' and on to absolutely brilliant numbers like 'Waterloo Sunset'. That Ray Davies is pure genius. However, the very best show I saw in the UK was on a Sunday in June last year when Hendrix, Cream and Procol Harem all appeared one after the other at the Saville Theatre in London. That show really blew my mind.'

'Bloody hell,' exclaimed Pete, looking at me. 'We gotta get ourselves over there soon.'

'Shit yeah,' I said with equal enthusiasm.

Pete, Barry and I jumped into Nobbys old rust bucket Holden as usual the next morning, but before we could say anything, he put up his hand and then tapped his watch.

'It's time for the next episode of Chicken Man,' said Nobby, reaching for the radio dial.

'What the fuck?' I began, but both Pete and Barry nudged me into silence. Within a few moments a serious sounding American male voice boomed out.

'Another exciting episode from the most fantastic crime fighter the world has ever known.'

This was followed by the sound of an assertive chicken announcing at high volume. 'BUCK, BUCK, BUCK, BUUUCK! CHICKEN MAN. Several excited female voices then added to the commotion by stating in unison, 'HE'S EVERYWHERE – HE'S EVERYWHERE! This nonsense continued for several more minutes with lines like, 'He'll be available to fight crime on weekends,' and 'Could someone get my rear zipper please,' followed after a slight pause by 'Hey watch it back there.'

We were all hooked. Listening to a type of calculated stupidity that took the piss out of other supposed comic book heroes was right up our alley and a great way to start the day. We loved it and frequently quoted lines from the show throughout the day to one another ('Good morning winged warrior', 'Say, aren't you the feathered fighter' etc.).

We all perspired and grunted our way through the heat as we continued to keep bricks and mud up to the demanding brickies, as the brick walls grew ever higher. The lumps of rubber from Kevin were indeed preventing my poor fingertips from too much more wear and tear from the constant picking up of bricks. What a godsend!

That night, Barry entertained us royally again with vivid descriptions of clothing that were considered fashionable in England when he was there. 'Well, colourful shirts are all the go,' he said helpfully. 'In fact, the paisley pattern has made a big comeback.'

'I don't like the sound of that,' I said, wrinkling up my nose in disgust. 'What about strides then?'

'Yep, hipsters with big buckle belts strategically situated over a bloke's pubic area are in big time,' enthused Barry. 'The best pants are cut as bell bottoms, with a huge flair at the bottom of each leg.'

Pete and I looked at each other with raised eyebrows. We were both thinking the same thing. Where could we get daks like that in Australia?

Suddenly Pete disappeared, returning a short while later with a copy of the Perth Yellow Pages phone directory that he had temporarily borrowed from the public phone box, down the street. All three of us pored over the book with considerable interest, eventually settling our eyes on an advertisement that boldly stated: 'Perth Tailor – Specialising in Carnaby Street Fashions.'

The shop was close to the centre of the Perth CBD.

'I'm going to see this bloke straight after work tomorrow,' beamed Pete, thrusting his index finger in the direction of the said ad.

'Me too,' shouted Barry and I in unison.

16

CARNABY STREET AUSSIE STYLE

At the end of another strenuous day playing with bricks, sand and cement, Kevin appeared amongst us with a wad of pay packets. I opened mine on the spot. You bloody beauty! $47 clear after tax.

'Yep,' said Pete. 'And when you work overtime on Saturday, you'll clear a bit over $60.'

'Even better,' I said with delight.

All three of us jumped on a bus that took us into the Perth CBD. Pete said he was going to the Commonwealth Bank to pay some of his wages into his account. I responded that I would open an account soon too and took off with Barry to find the tailor. We walked along Hay Street to the Plaza Arcade. Tucked away at the back was a small shop with a sign that indicated that it was run by A P Eckstein. Tailor - Specialist in Carnaby Street Fashions.

Upon entering the rather old-world style establishment, an immaculately dressed older man greeted us.

'Hello gentlemen – what may I do for you?'

After looking back over our shoulders to see that there was nobody else in the shop, we realised that the old bloke was actually talking to us. It seemed bizarre to be addressed so formally. Barry and I both looked more than a bit raggedy arsed.

Barry recovered first by advising Mister Eckstein that we each wanted a pair of Carnaby Street style trousers. The aged shopkeeper listened with great care to Barry's detailed description of the need for the said trousers to be low and hip hugging with 20-inch flared bottoms. He nodded his understanding, and with equal care took each of our measurements. I squirmed just a bit when he delicately took my inside leg measurement, but the old boy was the epitome of professionalism, and worked with supreme efficiency.

After establishing that Barry and I both wanted these new pants to be colourful, old Mister Eckstein showed us a range of truly impressive materials. Barry selected his from a bolt of royal blue cotton cloth, whilst I chose one of red crimson. To this point everything had gone smoothly.

I had previously only bought clothing off the shelf, and this highly efficient and polished service had me feeling rather special. Our expert provider of such polished civility brought the transaction to its inevitable end. 'Each pair will be $25,' he beamed to Barry and I leaving no room for us to back out. '$10 deposit with the balance payable next Friday, which is when you may pick them up,' he finished. I felt a bit numb as I passed over a brand new $10 note.

As Barry and I were walking back along Hay Street, I looked over at my new mate.

'Shit Barry, what have we done?'

'What do ya mean?' he asked.

'Well, I've never paid more than ten bucks for a pair of strides in my life, and I've just committed myself to buying a pair for $25 from an old guy who looks as though he's a hundred, and probably has no idea about modern fashion whatsoever,' I said feeling a bit amazed at my own impetuosity.

'Relax,' said Barry, looking calm and assured. 'I reckon we're going to be pleased with our decision. Let's go and have a beer.'

As we sat enjoying our second large pot of Swan draught at the Melbourne Hotel, Pete suddenly appeared, red faced and looking somewhat perplexed.

'What's up Pete?' I said to my obviously agitated mate.

'Well, I went to the tailor in the Plaza Arcade, and the old bloke in there assured me that you two blokes had given him a thorough briefing about the style of bell bottoms we were all after and took my measurements. I assumed you had negotiated a fair price, so I selected some heavy weight cherry red material without hesitation.'

'So, what's the problem?' asked Barry.

'Well, the old fart charged me the outrageous price of $28 for one pair of daks,' fumed Pete, turning and striding towards the bar to get himself a beer.

'Must have been the heavier material,' said Barry in a matter-of-fact tone.

Finally arriving back at Jonkers I was delighted to find another letter from my Mum had arrived. It was the first from her since I had left Yaringa.

It read:

> *Received your letter yesterday and glad to know that you made it safely back to Perth and are with Pete again. Can't see how you come to be broke on arrival in Perth. Surely there was nothing to spend your money on in the outback. Oh well, it's your business!*
>
> *Bobbie wore your jumper one day, so I washed it and put it away safely.*

By now I was quite accustomed to working six days a week. It felt natural to roll out of bed at 6am, throw on my work togs, swallow as much breakfast as was provided, and jump into Nobby's old Holden with Pete and Barry in time to hear another episode from the great Chicken Man on the car radio, before starting the daily grind.

We were sitting around at lunchtime enjoying our grub and the break from the hard physical grind, when the chat eventually and predictably found its way to the subject of the opposite sex. Some of the blokes certainly had some ribald stories to tell, although they were, at best exaggerated, and more often than not, probably complete fabrications. One older guy who, was known to us as Chocka, listened intently to the conversation with obvious interest. 'The best bird I ever had was a dancing girl from Manangatang,' he said with considerable relish.

'That's up in northern Victoria, isn't it?' asked Pete. 'What was her name?'

'Never found out properly,' replied Chocka. 'I just knew her as the Mallee Root,' he then said with a straight face, before quickly adding 'And she could squeeze my lemon till the juice ran down my leg'.

This additional line was delivered before most of us had even fully grasped the initial joke, and it was all executed with Chocka's poker face completely intact.

After the laughter eventually died down, I turned to our comedian buddy and asked, 'Where the hell did you get that last quote from mate, it's a pearler?'

'It's just a great line from an old blues song,' replied Chock. I always try to remember the sensitive and loving lyrics from some of the old blues masters,'

'So, who do you consider are some of the best bluesmen?' I asked.

'Oh, the usual like Howlin' Wolf and Muddy Waters. But my all-time favourite has to be Big Joe Turner'.

'Never heard of him,' said Pete. 'Who is he?'

'Well, you blokes may think that guys like Presley and Berry invented rock and roll, but for mine Big Joe was years ahead of them. You should try to catch up with his version of 'Shake, Rattle and Roll.' His take on that song made Bill Hailey's version sound like a nursery rhyme. In addition to that Big Joe came up with the immortal line of, *you can rock me baby till my face turns cherry red*', finished Chocka, eventually breaking into a beaming smile. I made a mental note to check out this Big Joe guy as soon as I got the chance.

As we drove back towards Mount Lawley, we passed a few small inner suburban parks where there were considerable congregations of First Australians gathered. They appeared to just be listlessly sitting around in groups. I hadn't seen this activity back in Melbourne, but come to think of it, we didn't seem to see many Indigenous people in Victoria, period. I made these observations to the others in the car.

Nobby was the first to reply.

'Nothin' ya can do with the bugger's mate,' he said. 'They don't last in any jobs, can't hold their grog, take lots of money from the government, and sit on their arses all day.' It was a hopeless and inaccurate diatribe, but we didn't know enough to dispute it. I tried to put it out of my mind, but the apparent victimisation of these people troubled me.

Inspired by the afternoon's enthusiastic references to blues music, Barry, Pete and I made our way that evening to the Galaxy Club in a cab. Chocka had told us that a great local blues band was performing there, and so we arrived with great anticipation. We weren't disappointed.

A young band by the name of the Jelly Roll Bakers captured our attention immediately with a loud blues vibe that had us all tapping our toes and nodding our heads, with almost complete abandon.

'They used to call themselves My Grandfathers Blues,' yelled an appreciative stranger to my left. 'They're bloody great,' I responded equally loudly. It was one of the few evenings out that we didn't bother chasing any birds at all. The music was enough.

WE HAD JUST FINISHED our Sunday breakfast when Pete and Barry introduced me to another Jonkers resident in the person of Uli.

'Uli has a car,' explained Pete. 'And he has suggested that we all head off to the beach for a swim.'

'Nice to meet you, Uli,' I said, observing a conservatively dressed guy who appeared about ten or so years older than Pete, Barry and I.

'Nice to meet you too,' Uli replied politely in a strong European accent I couldn't place. 'It will be nice to have you join us at the beach'.

We drove down through Fremantle, yacking about everything and anything, eventually stopping at Rockingham Beach.

We were all looking trim and tanned from the hard work in the hot Australian sun, so we felt pretty good as we strode down towards the golden sand. I had worked my way up to a fair strut by the time we got there. Our heads pivoted to and fro as we looked for admiring glances from the fairer sex. But instead, we only saw young families enjoying the sun and surf. The mums and dads took no notice of us as they concentrated on having fun with their kids.

'Nothing else to do but have a bloody good swim, and some sport,' announced the ever practical Barry, stripping quickly down to his togs, and grabbing a tennis ball. We spent the next hour or more throwing the ball to each other in a rudimentary game of keepings off that consisted mainly of pushing, shoving and laughing a lot.

After devouring a tasteless meat pie from a nearby milk bar, we jumped back into the car, and headed towards another beach.

'Waikiki is bound to have plenty of young chicks for us the frolic with,' enthused Pete. Alas, once again his prediction failed to bear fruit, so we walked our legs off along the sand expecting to find a bevy of young beauties further along the beach with whom to fraternise.

'Well, where the fuck do all the eligible birds go on a warm Sunday afternoon?' said my dejected mate, Pete.

Barry and I felt equally disappointed, and it was only Uli that appeared unaffected. 'Come on,' he said, attempting to lift our spirits. 'Let's head back to Fremantle for a few beers to finish off the day'.

'Only if you insist,' I replied over my shoulder, as I began to jog back to the car, followed at pace by the others.

We arrived at a pub that Uli knew well. He entered through a side door with us following close behind. We all signed a statutory declaration that we were all bona fide travellers and joined the apparently similarly certified group of other punters, all of whom were happily imbibing alcohol in the public bar that late Sunday afternoon in Fremantle.

We arrived back at Jonkers quite late, slightly worse for wear, but in extremely high spirits, until we found out that we had missed dinner by some hours. It took us some time to find a fish and chip shop that was open. It was great grub.

SHORTLY AFTER ARRIVING at the building site the next day, the foreman Kevin took me aside.

'I've got a special job for you today son,' he said in a not unfriendly tone, while marching us towards a device that I hadn't seen in use during the previous week.

'This here's a brick cutting machine,' he said standing in front of a mechanical device.

It consisted of a flat tray at waist height and stood on four sturdy metal legs with a cylindrical cutting blade hovering above it.

Kevin pressed a button that set the cylinder spinning. He slapped a brick on the tray, held it in place with his left hand, and brought down the head containing the spinning cutting blade on to the brick, cutting it in half. The noise was deafening. 'Reckon you can do that?' asked Kevin.

'I'll give it a go boss,' I said with an unconvincing light heartedness.

A big, complex machine like that made me nervous. My ever-present clumsiness could result in the loss of some vital personal appendage.

'Good,' replied Kevin. 'Start with cutting a hundred in half, and then two hundred in three quarter and one quarter sections,' he finished, striding off to provide further guidance elsewhere.

Cripes. He didn't even wait to see if I could manage.

Nevertheless, throwing caution to wind, I began my new task, and before long I was cutting and stacking the brick sections with a surprisingly accuracy. I did however notice that I found it difficult to clearly hear my mates talking during the lunch break. Was I going deaf?

As we were returning to Mount Lawley that afternoon, Pete spoke loudly to our partially deaf driver mate Nobby (he'd probably worked the brick cutter at some stage too).

'Could you drop me off in Lord Street, Highgate tonight mate?'

'Sure thing,' yelled Nobby at an even greater volume.

'What are you up to Pete?' I asked.

'You'll know soon enough,' he replied, as he opened the car door.

'Well don't be late for dinner again,' I responded in my best high pitched motherly impersonation.

After dinner, Pete dragged Uli's semi portable record player into the lounge room, plugged it in, and disappeared back to the bedroom. He reappeared a short time later, reverently holding an LP record.

'I have Dylan's latest and best recording – John Wesley Harding,' said Pete, triumphantly holding up the record in its cardboard sleeve for all to see.

I squinted at the light brown cover featuring a picture of four nondescript males.

'I haven't heard this album before – any good?'

'Any fucking good?' gasped Pete. 'This bloke is the closest thing there is a musical god, and you ask me if it's any bloody good.'

'I reckon the fella sings through his nose a good bit,' said Barry, joining in the sport.

'Shut up and just listen,' replied Pete indignantly placing the needle on the spinning disc.

By the time we had sat listening through the likes of 'I Dreamed I Saw St Augustine', 'All Along the Watchtower' and 'The Wicked Messenger', we were all enthralled. As the last breezy notes to 'I'll Be Your Baby Tonight' concluded, Barry looked over at me.

'I s'pose we should listen to it one more time, just to confirm that it is a piece of musical shit,' he grinned at me and winked.

Pete took no notice. He knew that we were all hooked. He had already turned the record over and was in the process of returning the needle to track one once again, without the slightest intention of asking permission. It was fine by us. What an album.

It was back to carting bricks in the hot sun again the next day. The pace was furious as always, with the brickies' demands for speedier deliveries of bricks and mortar becoming ever more frequent.

Finally, the inevitable happened. Pete and I watched in horror as Barry ran flat out along the wooden board, pushing an overloaded barrow of bricks. He lost his footing causing he and the barrow to veer off track and abruptly end their high-speed journey in a freshly dug trench. Pete and I stopped what we were doing and raced over to our mate. 'You okay Barry?' yelled Pete.

Barry rolled over and sprang to his feet with great athleticism, roaring in a loud and most indignant voice, 'Enough, enough she cried, as she waved her wooden leg.'

Pete and I stopped running in an instant and spontaneously burst out with surprised laughter.

The relatively unhurt Barry joined in with the laughter.

'What the fuck did you just say?' chortled Pete.

'It's just a saying that my old uncle used when he was exasperated,' grinned Barry.

Temperatures slowly rose throughout the day on the work site. To make matters worse Pete, Barry and I were amongst a group of labourers who were directed to commence digging deep trenches for new footings on an adjacent block of land. Much of Perth has been built on sand, or at least very sandy soil. This location was no exception. Often one would throw out a shovel full of sand, only to have two shovels full fall back in the trench. We were hot, frustrated, and at times extremely short tempered.

The phrase 'Enough, enough she cried' had a good airing that day. No matter how frequently we left the trench to pour tepid water from a hose down our parched throats, we couldn't seem to sate our thirsts.

'Can you drop us off at our local pub tonight, please Nobby?' asked Pete as we were driving home from work.

'Sure thing guys,' responded our ever obliging driver. 'I might just have a couple of pots with you'.

After speedily sinking three pots of chilled amber fluid each, our moods brightened considerably.

'Hey, we better get going,' said the ever-attentive Barry.

'If we don't leave now, we'll miss dinner at Bonkers (Jonkers).'

Reluctantly we made our way out of the pub, making it just in time for our evening meal at the boarding house.

'I've still got a bloody big thirst, guys,' announced Pete after our meal. 'Fancy going back for a few more beers?'

'Not me,' replied Barry sensibly. 'If I go back, I'd get fully pissed for sure, and we have to dig more bloody trenches tomorrow.'

'Weak as piss,' I said. 'C'mon Pete, let's just have a couple more pots.'

'Aw just a couple then,' he replied.

Off we sauntered with intent.

I WOKE up at 5.30 am with a raging thirst and swollen tongue. The hilarity and laughter from the previous evening were merely a blur. I staggered to the toilet to relieve my close to exploding bladder. Pete waited impatiently outside the door, evidently with the same condition.

After splashing water on to our faces we tottered into the breakfast room to roars of derisive laughter from the other boarding house inmates.

'Looks like you two drop kicks really tied one on last night,' said one uncaring and supposedly witty punter.

We just managed to keep some toast and tea down before Barry brightly told us that Nobby would be waiting for us outside in two minutes. We made it – but only just and were soon back on the shovels again as the temperature began to slowly rise. Sweat oozed out of every pore of my skin and judging from the slowly moving apparition digging further up the trench, Pete was doing it just as tough.

On the other hand, Barry seemed untroubled as he wielded his shovel without difficulty, chatting amiably to everyone around him.

'I've been told that it's a mistake to drink too much alcohol when you're really thirsty,' he said loudly to nobody in particular. 'Bloody stuff just dehydrates you more'.

'Fuck off,' I croaked, as I walked slowly to the water hose for the tenth time that morning. It took till well after lunch before I began to feel human again. How many bloody pots *did* I drink the night before?

Four o clock couldn't come quickly enough for all of us. We collected our pay packets, and there was indeed just over $60 in mine, as my mates had prophesised. We only just remembered to thank Kevin before dashing off to the bus stop and jumping aboard a bus into the CBD.

OLD MISTER ECKSTEIN was there to greet us with the same extraordinary manners that he had displayed on our first visit.

'Gentlemen,' he beamed. 'Your custom-tailored trousers are all finished and ready for you to pick up.'

We grabbed the proffered brown paper parcels and scurried off to the changing rooms. Eagerly unwrapping my parcel, I saw my crimson-coloured pants nestled in the brown paper.

I stepped into them. Wow! They hugged my hips low, and the flared bell bottoms looked sensational. I burst out of my change room at the same moment as Barry. His royal blue pair looked equally impressive. We grinned at each other like a couple of kids at Christmas, before rushing over to the section of the shop displaying leather belts. I found a black three inch belt with a large buckle, and threaded it through my trouser loops, before standing admiringly in front of a full length mirror.

Barry excitedly pushed me to one side to stand in my place. We looked at each other smiling broadly.

'Fucking fantastic,' I said excitedly.

'What do you guys think of these?' said a voice from the far end of the store.

Pete had been trying his new daks on as well. We turned around and gasped. Pete's bell bottoms set a new standard in male clothing elegance, eclipsing even our stylish new strides. Pete's pair had been made from heavier material that glowed a deep cherry red colour.

'Jeepers Pete,' I said. 'Your bell bottoms seem to flare even more than ours.'

'I went for broke and ordered 22-inch cuffs,' he explained.

'Well, you've created the hippest threads in Perth for sure,' enthused Barry. I nodded my agreement cheerfully.

'Can't wait till we hit the nights spots in these,' I said punching the air.

Throughout these exchanges Mister Eckstein, watched on with a smile. The man was truly dedicated to his craft. He took the balance of our payments and carefully placed the banknotes in the till. Each of us stepped lightly out of that highly skilled gentleman's shop that evening.

17

CASANOVA

We couldn't wait to wear our fancy new strides out in Perth. We were sure that no one in that fair city had ever seen anything like them.

We shampooed our hair, selected our best shirts to match the new bell bottoms, and slipped into our newly acquired, chick-enticing togs.

Pinocchio's nightclub didn't open until late, so we made our way to the Melbourne Hotel, striding confidently into the public bar. Our appearance quickly solicited some loud wolf whistles from many of the exclusively male punters, accompanied by some sarcastic comments that would have severely embarrassed any less confident young blokes. 'I think I'll shag the one in blue strides first,' enthused one large burly worker.

'Nah, I'm going for the long-haired blonde one in red daks,' slurred his mate. 'He looks more like a Sheila to me.'

'Fucking philistines,' barked Pete loudly, turning his back on our tormenters. This simply brought on additional howls of laughter from those at the bar.

We removed ourselves and headed for the more refined atmosphere of the saloon bar. While the beer in here would cost a bit more, the move quickly appeared to be a smart one. As I brought the first beer up to my mouth, I was sure I noticed some admiring glances from some classy looking dames at the other end of the bar. I nudged Barry and nodded discretely in the direction of the group of females.

Pete was still fuming about the pricks in the bar so didn't immediately pick up on the exchange.

'Bloody hell Bruce, they're about 10 or 15 years older than us,' said Barry.

'Think of the experience,' I murmured back and strode over to say hello to the ladies, leaving my mates to continue their anguish over the public bar buffoons.

My conversation with the four femme fatales was both intriguing and costly. Each of the ladies engaged in conversation with me in a most friendly manner as I bought several expensive rounds of Pimm's No 1 cup with lemonade. Within a short while all four were flirting with me with varying degrees of intensity.

'Bloody hell,' I thought conceitedly to myself. 'Is it my new bell bottoms, or just my tanned good looks?' Pete and Barry continued their conversations with some other blokes at the bar for some reason, ignoring my obvious steady progress.

Eventually a particularly flirty red head turned to me, looked me straight in eye, and said, 'Listen Bruce, we're sorry, but we all have a prior engagement tonight that we can't invite you to. However, all four of us are going to the drive-in movies tomorrow night, and we'd love to have you join us?'

Would I bloody ever.

We settled on a pickup time, and I gave the red head my address at Jonkers. I received a lingering kiss on the cheek from each of the ladies as they left. In addition, a blonde with a plunging neckline added a knowing wink and suggestive smile said, 'See *you* tomorrow night then Bruce.'

I sauntered back to join Pete and Barry. 'No good then mate?' queried Pete.

'Oh, I did okay,' I replied. 'I'm going to the drive-in tomorrow night with them.' 'What all bloody four of them?' gasped Barry.

'Yep,' I replied, trying unsuccessfully to hide my rather too obvious smirk. 'They'll eat you alive,' Barry predicted.

'With a bit of luck.'

Pinocchio's was a real hoot that night. Two bands were going to perform, starting with a group with the unlikely name of The Ingrown Toenail (they must have been up all night to think up that one).

Despite the adverse nomenclature, the boys knew how to rock, culminating their performance with a twenty-minute version of Deep Purple's 'Hush.'

Dance partners weren't hard to find as we grooved energetically and sung NAH NANA NAH NUNA NAH NUNA NAH at the top of our lungs.

They were replaced by The Current Bun. A very polished group of accomplished musos who kept the joint swinging until closing time. I confined my activities to dancing and drinking, figuring that I needed to save my erotic charms for the following night.

BARRY AND PETE had already begun to spread the news with the other boarders that Casanova Lowery had a solo date with four birds at a drive-in that night, so there was a bit of a buzz and some fruity innuendo over breakfast. I did my best to act cool, pretending that the event was nothing unusual for me.

Uli again kindly offered to drive us to the beach, suggesting that this time we opt for the closer location of Scarborough. After a good swim we found a decent café that made fresh sandwiches and pretty good coffee.

We then returned to the beach to eat lunch and take in the sights of numerous chicks in their bikinis. This beach was proving far better viewing value than either Rockingham or Waikiki.

As we sat chatting and joking, I began to withdraw from the conversation. I was getting a bit nervous about my planned sojourn with the four women that night. How was one bloke supposed to begin an amorous approach to four separate females simultaneously, particularly within the confines of an automobile? I tried to imagine various scenarios, but none seemed to make much sense.

Should I allow the girls to simply take the lead? No, my male ego demanded that I should set the scene and begin making the romantic advances. But how? After picking up a six pack of ouzo and cola on the way back we eventually returned to Jonkers in time for dinner without me forming any definitive plan of action. My slightly nervous state wasn't improving much.

At the appointed hour I strode out the front door of Jonkers, freshly showered, bathed in Old Spice after shave, and wearing my lucky red bell bottoms. As I walked down the front path, grasping my six pack of ouzo and colas, I couldn't help but notice two of Jonkers inmates surreptitiously peaking around the corner of the house, obviously checking to see if my solo night out with four attractive birds was actually true.

A green Valiant sedan pulled up punctually at the kerb with its windows down. Several of my dates poked their heads out.

'Woohoo Brucie,' yelled the redhead.

She jumped out of the back door and ushered me in to sit on the back seat. I obeyed without hesitation, and just managed to give a little wave to the open-mouthed guys at the side of the house, as I was squeezed in between the red head and the blonde. We were off!

The girls were in high spirits.

'Good boy!' shouted the front seat passenger. 'I see you've brought some booze along. What delights await us?'

'Aw just a few ouzos,' I replied. 'Hope you girls like it?'.

'We'll drink just about anything with alcohol in it,' bellowed back the bird from the front. 'We've got a few vodkas and whatever's too, so we won't go dry.'

These were girls after my own heart.

As we joined the queue to enter the drive-in, I looked at the illuminated sign displaying the features being shown that night. We were going to have the dubious pleasure of watching 'Dracula: Prince of Darkness'.

The second feature didn't sound a great deal more encouraging. 'The Plague of the Zombies' failed to immediately conjure up images of shared romantic embraces between four birds and a solo male in a Valiant sedan that night.

'Hope you like our selection of movies,' said the blonde on my right (who pleasingly was again proudly displaying considerable cleavage). We all love supernatural flicks that either give us a fright, or if they're poorly made, give us a chance to have a bloody good laugh.'

'Both movies look great,' I lied.

As soon as we parked the Valiant, I offered each of the girls a can of ouzo which was quickly accepted. Soon the credits began to role. Apparently, this mighty epic had been filmed in Techniscope, whatever that meant, and starred the master of horror himself, Christopher Lee. The film opened with a priest chastising another priest for wishing to dispose of a woman's corpse as if it were a vampire, reminding everyone that Dracula had been destroyed 10 years previously.

Nevertheless, while visiting an inn in the next scene, the supposedly wise priest still warns four obviously naive young English tourists not to visit Karlsbad. Naturally enough, for the sake of the narrative, the four tourists are not merely naïve, but bloody stupid as well. Somehow, they find themselves in a driverless coach that takes them to (yes, you guessed it) a particularly spooky looking castle, where they discover a dinner table set for four. Before long one of the idiot tourists visits the castle crypt where he is violently murdered by a bloke named Klove, who then mixes his blood with Dracula's ashes. I decided this was the right time to make my first move.

Turning to face the blonde beside me, I quietly whispered some poorly worded platitudes that made a vain attempt to flatter her good looks.

'Shit,' cried the redhead on the other side of our bench seat in a loud voice. 'Bloody Dracula's going to be revived.'

The blonde reacted to the redhead's comment with a loud 'Oh no,' completely ignoring my gentle attempt at verbal foreplay.

After watching Christopher Lee hissing (he had no dialogue in the film whatsoever) his way around the castle, I turned my attention this time to the redhead, and again tried to whisper some persuasive words that were designed to flatter, if not arouse some passion.

'Look!' cried the blonde loudly on the other side of me, as she grasped my arm forcefully. 'He's gonna bite her neck.' I was sure I heard the additional sound of a suppressed snigger from the front seat. This game of poorly attempted seduction on my part, followed by immediate and decisive distraction by one, or more, of the non-targeted females, continued throughout the entire first movie. So much so that I was frankly relieved when I witnessed frigging Christopher Lee's Dracula finally sinking and drowning in the castle's freezing moat.

During the interval, I offered to buy everyone some cooked chips. They were barely warm by the time I got back to the car. This was reciprocated with an offer of a slightly warmer can of Vodka and orange that was thrust into my hand. I hoped that the heat of passion in the car for the second feature was going to be hotter than the chips and vodka.

The girl in the front passenger seat had swapped with the blonde in the back seat, saying that the blonde would have a better view of the second movie.

I couldn't help but notice that her replacement had an impressive amount of red lipstick on her full lips.

Maybe this will be my opportunity.

The second feature got underway as I drained my can of Vodka and whatever. The new flick promised an even more distasteful degree of horror, with voodoo ceremonies and the plague in an 1860's Cornish village. To add to the general pandemonium, there were a high number of hideous looking zombies wandering about (apparently some bastard had brought a truly evil black magic formula back from Haiti).

I turned towards the owner of the aforementioned large red lips and whispered something suggestive. The response was a horrendously loud sneeze. It brought howls of laughter from the other three females in the vehicle.

'Good one Janet,' called someone from the front of the cabin.

I waited for things to settle down, trying not to watch the gruesome images flickering on the screen, but all of the girls had the giggles by now.

Every ghastly twist in the story, initiated gales of highly audible contractions of the girl's diaphragms. It seemed that they were almost out of control with horror induced mirth. My relief was once again palpable when eventually the baddies all died horrible deaths in a fiery inferno, and the laughter in the car finally died away too.

All four girls chatted away with me in the same flirty way as before, all the way back to Mount Lawley. As we pulled up at the kerb, red lips leaned over and gave me a seriously full on pash, which included the vigorous use of her probing tongue. I suddenly experienced a rush of blood to the penile area.

'See ya later, Brucie,' said the redhead, stepping out of the car, indicating that it was time for me to leave the vehicle. I blinked at red lips who smiled seductively back at me mouthing,

'See you soon Bruce'.

I left the girl's company in a rather bewildered state, but even so, still couldn't help but notice some rather obvious high fiving going on inside the car as it roared away. My excited penis subsided to its previous limp state as I slowly walked back into the boarding house, wondering what the hell had just happened to me.

It was only after I had lain awake for a good hour or so that I finally realised that those four women had taught me some valuable life lessons that night. Chief amongst them was to learn some genuine respect towards the opposite sex, and the other was to limit my romantic advances to one female at a time.

18

TEMPTING FATE

The guys hung on my every word the next morning during breakfast. I took a casual stand, stating that being a gentleman, I couldn't possibly incriminate any of my drive-in loving female friends.

What the blokes didn't know wouldn't hurt them, and in any case, I was rather pleased with my newly acquired 'Casanova' status, even if reality dictated otherwise.

It was back on the shovels again hoisting sandy soil from a seemingly never-ending trench. As usual we resorted to much silly humour as possible to get us through the day.

After dinner that night, Pete, Barry and I sat chatting about our various travel adventures. Naturally it was mainly Barry who led the discussion again, having travelled extensively overseas already. England was still at the forefront of our minds, so Barry talked a great deal about the delights of Pommie pubs, English beer, the sites of London, and again the plentiful supply of birds who just loved guys from the Antipodes. However, it was when he began to elaborate about his time in Sweden, that our ears pricked up considerably. The blonde-haired and blue-eyed chicks there were apparently a great deal freer with their favours than anywhere else in the world. My ears burnt a good bit with some of Barry's detailed tales of high Scandinavian eroticism.

'Okay, let's start making some serious plans to travel there together,' said Pete. 'But we all need to do some serious saving for the fare.'

'D'ya reckon it's better to go by boat or plane?' I asked Barry.

'Definitely by boat,' he replied. 'It's a lot of fun on board, and again a lot of girls are likely to be more friendly at sea than on dry land, for some reason.' This was getting more and more interesting by the minute. Nonstop debauchery beckoned. The lessons learnt from the evening before quickly evaporating within my brain. We finished the nights discussions by making a pact that as soon as we had saved up sufficient money, the three of us would be off to Europe together for the adventure of a lifetime.

After another hard day at work, I arrived back to find a letter from Gil. His frankness about a meeting and conversation with Trish really hit me hard.

> 'I bumped into Trish, and she only wanted to talk about you. She said she was being severely restricted by her family in everything she did, but that she was determined to marry you despite the pressure being put on her. That girl really loves and misses you real bad man. If there is a wedding, I'd like to be your best man'.

It seemed that she was really trying to find a way to write to me, though alas without success. Also, it wasn't entirely clear if my letters to her were getting through. I had no doubt that Trish was being held against her will, but one thing appeared certain.

She loved me deeply and was hurting from our enforced separation. I had to do something.

After our evening meal, I grabbed Pete for a confidential chat in the back garden. My agitated state had elevated to genuine anguish about what may be happening to Trish back in Melbourne.

'I think I have to go back to Melbourne to help her,' I said. I was quite emotional.

'But what do you think you'll achieve, mate? Her family, and from the sound of it, the cops are going to stop you seeing her.'

'We could run away together.'

'But you have no money saved, so where would you go, and how could you look after her?'

'We'll find a way,' I said stubbornly.

'Well, I think you need to calm down and sleep on it overnight.

But I didn't sleep much at all. I fretted about Trish constantly, tossing and turning in my narrow bed as half a dozen tired blokes around me snored away, oblivious to my dilemma.

After a hot and busy workday on the shovels, Pete suggested we go and have a chat at a pub near the boarding house. My mood had not improved throughout the day from the night before. I was bone tired too.

The more I thought about Gil's letter, the more I felt that I had to go back to Melbourne to save Trish.

We sat in silence in the pub bar as we downed our first pot of beer. Eventually Pete broached the obviously delicate subject.

'Have you thought any more about returning to Melbourne early?' he asked.

'Yep,' I replied, offering no further information.

'Well, apart from what I said last night about questioning how successful you could possibly be by trying to elope with Trish, you'll be walking away from a very well paid job here, and our plans to go to Europe together would have to be put off indefinitely.'

'Fuck me Pete,' I cried. 'Don't you understand that my love for Trish is more important to me than anything else in my life?'

Pete's eyes narrowed.

'Well mate, for a guy so desperately in love with your girl, you spend a helluva lot of time chasing skirt,' he said.

'Fuck off.'

I stepped off my bar stool and walked out of the bar.

Pete and I remained civil to one another over breakfast and on the job throughout the morning, but there was an uneasy tension between us from our disagreement the day before. It was Barry who attempted to break the ice when, after we'd eaten our lunch, and had lit up a fag each, said.

'C'mon you two, enough is enough. You need to kiss and make up.'

'I've made up my mind,' I said obstinately. 'I'm off to buy a ticket back to Melbourne straight after work today.'

Silence followed my announcement for what seemed an eternity, before Pete looked me straight in the eye and said, 'Okay mate. If you feel that strongly about the matter, I'll support you fully in whatever way I can. I still think you're making a big mistake, but you have my backing regardless.'

'Thanks, I appreciate it.'

All three of us then sat smoking in silence, as each of us started to think about how my sudden change of plan would affect each of us.

After work I caught a bus into the Perth CBD and quickly found a travel agent.

'What's the best and quickest way to buy a ticket to Melbourne?' I asked the pleasant looking woman behind the counter.

'Well, the cheapest and quickest would be a nonstop bus

straight into Melbourne CBD,' she replied immediately. 'There's one leaving on Saturday morning at 8.30am, and a ticket will set you back you $35.'

'Then I'd like to buy a ticket for one please,' I said without hesitation. It was the quickest of transactions for such a major trip.

After dinner that evening I showed Pete and Barry my ticket.

'Shit that soon,' said Pete. 'I've made up my mind to follow you back to Melbourne, but can I ask you to try to sort things out with Trish by staying in Melbourne until I get there, so we can return to the Hills together?'

'Sure thing,' I replied.

I knew that completing a big home coming together was important to my mate, and I felt the same way. 'I can book myself into a week's accommodation somewhere near the city before going home. However, if Trish is game, I may take off north with her straight away without going home,' I said, fully revealing my complete lack of logical planning.

'I've decided to fly back to New Zealand to catch up with my family,' said Barry. But I still intend to then fly back to OZ within a few months, before going back to Europe. Depending on how things work out for you guys, I'd still love for the three of us to travel overseas together, but I do understand your commitment to your girl Bruce.'

Things were changing fast, with both mates making considerable changes to their plans in the hope that I would still travel with them to Europe.

As soon as I arrived at work, I made my way over to see the boss Kevin and told him that an emergency at home meant that I had to pass in my notice. I would depart Perth on Saturday morning.

'Okay young man,' he said, looking me in the eye. 'You've

been a hard worker, so there's always a job back here for you if you return. Good luck son'.

I worked harder than ever on that final day to show Kevin the total respect that I genuinely felt for him.

After dinner that evening, Pete, Barry and I went to a local pub for a few farewell beers. It was clear that all three of us were feeling a bit blue. I'd only known Barry for a few weeks, but sometimes friendships between people blossom and firm up quickly, and this had been the case between the two of us. And here I was again splitting up with my close mate and staunch ally Pete. And all due to my own personal decisions, made under a huge emotional cloud.

We chatted away, managing to still find some things to laugh about, although the humour was more than a bit forced. In the back of our minds, we were all wondering how the hell would things work out.

That night, I lay wide awake. The events of the past few months swirled through my head. The many adventures had been exhilarating to say the least. Travelling had certainly worked its way into my blood, but my feelings for Trish obscured everything else. For the first time since reading Gil's letter, doubts entered my mind. Would Trish agree to run away with me? If so, how could I look after all her needs? Would we indefinitely be on the run from the police? I clenched my fists. Fuck it!

I had to try. I would see what happened when I got to Melbourne.

POSTSCRIPT

My old close travelling mate Peter Lawrance now lives in Canberra, but we are still in regular contact by phone and continue our never-ending dialogue about the ways of the world.

Gil Halliday is happily married to his wife Kath. They have been married for over fifty years and live five kilometres from my place in Sassafras. We still meet up for coffee to reminisce about the old days.

Regrettably, big Bob Manders and my paths never crossed again after our time together in '68. My last vision of him waving in my general direction from the work truck that morning so long ago will be stuck in my memory forever.

I continued to correspond with Barry Brogan after he returned to New Zealand and again when he eventually returned to Australia as he readied himself for another overseas jaunt. Our correspondence petered out after that.

Steve Harris and I still text each other regularly, usually about similar themes to the letters he sent to us in O'Malley.

O'Malley Railway Camp hasn't been manned for many decades. It's very difficult to get to, but I must try someday.

Postscript

Recent research while writing this book has revealed the tall stories about Italian POW's being used as fettlers during WW2 has turned out the be absolutely correct. Around 300 spent many months working around Cook, O'Malley and Fisher with their compliment of NCO's and guards. Another recently revealed astounding fact that 'set me on my heels' was the fact that O'Malley is located uncomfortably close to Maralinga. If that name rings a bell, I'm not surprised. Maralinga was the site where the British Military detonated four nuclear bombs as a test in 1956, a mere twelve years before we were there (this may give us a clue about the unusual behaviour of our Ganger back then?).

Yaringa still exists as a working sheep station. Somewhat surprisingly, I found that it now boasts a camping ground by the sea for travellers, complete with flushing toilets, Telstra mobile coverage and a barbeque area incorporating a pizza oven, if you don't mind!

I saw the great Johnny O'Keefe live a second time in 1971 at the Dorset Gardens Hotel in Croydon, Victoria. He was equally electrifying that night. He passed away in October 1978 at the all too young age of 43. He touched my life again in 2008 when my daughter Brooke played the part of his second wife in the stage musical, 'Shout – The Legend of the Wild One', which toured most of Australia to wide acclaim.

ACKNOWLEDGMENTS

The author wishes to thank his great mate Geoff Rowcroft and publisher Jessica Mudditt of Hembury Books for their untiring work in copy editing this manuscript into its final published state.

A special thanks go to my wife Sue, who has provided so much support throughout our married life.

ALSO BY BRUCE LOWERY

Did you enjoy reading *Catch the Wind*?

Please visit Bruce Lowery's website for updates on the forthcoming sequel, *Out of Time*, which is scheduled for release in 2025.

www.brucelowery.com

www.ingramcontent.com/pod-product-compliance
Lightning Source LLC
Chambersburg PA
CBHW031411290426
44110CB00011B/344